Love Feast

Love Feast

Together at the Table

MARTHA JOHNSON BOURLAKAS

Morehouse Publishing
NEW YORK

Morehouse Publishing, 19 East 34th Street, New York, NY 10016
Morehouse Publishing is an imprint of Church Publishing Incorporated.
www.churchpublishing.org

Cover design by Laurie Klein Westhafer
Interior design and typesetting by Beth Oberholtzer Design

Library of Congress Cataloging-in-Publication Data

A record of this book is available from the Library of Congress.
ISBN-13: 978-0-8192-3213-7 (pbk.)
ISBN-13: 978-0-8192-3214-4 (ebook)

Printed in the United States of America

Contents

V

Love Feast is dedicated with deepest love
to Mark, Hannah, Sarah, Elizabeth,
to my parents, Margie and John,
and with gratitude for my constant
writing companion Sammy.

INTRODUCTION
Grace

Grace was a word I had never fully considered until I began this book. It wasn't until I was nearly finished that my husband Mark pointed me to Frederick Buechner's definition:

> Grace is something you can never get but only be given. The grace of God means something like: Here is your life. You might never have been, but you are because the party wouldn't have been complete without you. Here is the world. Beautiful and terrible things will happen. Don't be afraid. I am with you. Nothing can ever separate us. It's for you I created the universe. I love you. There's only one catch. Like any other gift, the gift of grace can be yours only

if you reach out and take it. Maybe being able
to reach and take it is a gift too.[1]

Church has always been part of my life. Even
during times when I've wanted to escape—and
there have been plenty—to escape the church
would be to escape my heart. I married a man who
became an Episcopal priest and is now a bishop. As
Mark's heart is inextricably connected to mine, I do
not want to leave the church so I might as well pull
up a pew and stay put. I have proceeded stubbornly
at times, but I have finally grown into the rhythm
of this spiritual journey, this life in God. Where I
have predicted the path would be narrow or dog-
matic, I have encountered endless alternate routes.
Where I have expected quick, simple answers to my
pleading prayers, I have experienced God's wide,
expansive breathing and listening space. Where I
have expected scarcity of forgiveness or love, I have
found an abundance of grace.

In the last twenty years, I have participated in
and led many spirituality groups. Most of these

---

1. Frederick Buechner, *Wishful Thinking: A Seeker's ABC*
(New York: Harper Collins Publishers, 1993), 39.

groups are female, but some are co-ed and I hear common themes in almost every gathering:

I miss connecting with God, but I'm so busy with meetings, appointments and taking care of others that my spiritual needs fall to the bottom.

I really don't know where I am on my spiritual journey. I just know I want to walk with others and learn from their stories.

I don't understand why the spiritual life seems like it has to be serious. I wish there were more room for fun and delight.

I feel guilty because I don't pray or worship enough. I need to be a better believer, a better person.

I pray that *Love Feast* will serve as a guide for some of these concerns. I do not presume to have some kind of inside track on the spiritual path. I most definitely do not. I do not presume my story is more significant or meaningful than yours because God knows many of you have much more exciting or traumatic life stories than mine. What I intend to do is encourage the sharing of our spiritual stories with each other. While we don't need to wallow in our circumstances, sharing the pain, energy, and growth of our stories enables us to become more compassionate, more connected, more whole. In truth, maybe a little wallowing does us all some good. I hope you will read my words and then share your own, either written and spoken, and on and on and on.

Over and over I hear women say, before sharing something personal or painful, "My life is easy compared to what my friend, [mom, sister, daughter, etc.] is going through." This expression is such an acknowledgment of the shared pain in the world and sympathy for other women's experiences, crucial for our global healing. The resistance to self-pity can enable us to move forward with hope, instead of standing still in shock. At the same time, I think we also hear our own mothers', grandmothers' and great-grandmothers' voices saying, "Don't get the big-head. There's always somebody who has it worse than you do." We feel we have to minimize our own experiences so we don't step on any toes, hog the emotional space.

I pray you come to know that, as wonderful as your mother and grandmother were or are, you don't have to worry about getting the big-head. There is plenty of mud for wallowing and you can always take a shower later. I don't want you to wait until you have more money or more space or your kids are grown, or your job is different or your book is finished to find God in *this* world, rather than waiting for the next. I hope you will laugh and spill coffee all over these pages. I hope that *Love Feast* will be a spiritual celebration of God's grace, complexity, and love. An acknowledgment that no matter who we are now or what we have done in the past, we all deserve and need to sit down at the *same* table, light the candles, and share God's abundant feast.

Love Feast

Crumbs, coffee, sugar, bread, milk, mugs, chewing, slurping, singing, spilling, visiting, laughing, feasting. The Love Feast, a ritual meal based on the ancient Christian agape meal, occurs several times a year during Moravian worship. While the Eucharist, the sacrament of Christ's body and blood, focuses on the relationship between God and humans, celebrating our redemption in Christ and Christ's presence in our lives, the Moravian Love Feast continues the Eucharistic blessing and celebration by connecting humans with each other so that for a few minutes, we may see Christ in each other—even the dirty, difficult other. The other who is spewing curse words. The other who is sitting in a wheelchair. The other who is crying. The other who is laughing. The other who is myself.

While the organist plays hymns, such as *Morning Star, O Cheering Sight,* for the choir and the congregation to sing, the Dieners, or corps of servers, distribute the sweet buns and coffee to everyone in the congregation. Made with mashed potatoes, flour, sugar, lemon juice, lemon and orange zests, the Love Feast bun is a cross between a sweet roll and a hamburger bun. The coffee, served in narrow white mugs, is about two-thirds sugar and milk. After everyone is served, all pray the Moravian grace: *Come, Lord Jesus, our guest to be /and bless these gifts bestowed by Thee. Amen.* Following the blessing, the feasting begins. Everyone remains seated to avoid chaos, but it is a time for sharing food and conversation with your neighbor. A way to bring together the sacred of God with the earthly pleasures of humanity. A symbol of the bounteous hospitality of God and the infinite possibilities for our own hospitality toward others.

When I was fifteen years old, I sat in a wooden pew of the Home Moravian Church, established in 1771, in Winston-Salem, North Carolina, and looked at the round sugary bun I held in one hand and the white mug of sugary, milky coffee in the other. I didn't know what to do with either because this was my first time in a Moravian Church. Having grown up in a straight-laced Southern Presbyterian church, I knew I was breaking at least one God-rule, if not several. Church was no place for messes, talking, spilling, sugar, laughter, food, noise, movement, enjoyment.

I didn't know then that the Love Feast would become a metaphor in my life but I knew from that day those two words belonged together. Over time I came to understand that this feast of love was the whole point of the spiritual journey. God, instead of being separate or distant from our unkempt, needy, imperfect selves, is right there beside us, holding the napkin, wiping our chins, tearing off bites of bread, moving us forward into the world.

Moravian Love Feast Bun Recipe
Adapted from Winkler Bakery Recipe

Winkler is the original Moravian bakery still in operation, in Old Salem, North Carolina, since 1800. Bakers still use the wood stove for all their baking.

INGREDIENTS

1 cup hot mashed potatoes, unseasoned, without milk or butter
$^1/_2$ cup scalded milk
1 cup sugar
$^1/_2$ cup butter, room temperature
2 eggs, beaten
$1^1/_2$ pounds flour
$^1/_4$ tsp nutmeg
2 packages yeast
$^1/_2$ cup warm water
2 Tbsps. orange rind, grated
2 Tbsps. lemon rind, grated
2 Tbsps. orange juice
1 Tbsp. lemon juice
$^1/_2$ tsp. mace

DIRECTIONS

1. Cream butter and sugar; add potatoes, mix well. Add lukewarm milk, then eggs, mix well.

2. Dissolve yeast in warm water and add to mixture.

3. Combine seasonings and rind. Add enough flour to make a soft dough.

4. Knead on a well-floured surface. Form into ball, place in a greased bowl. Cover with a cloth and let rise in a warm place until double in size.

5. Punch down; let rise again five to ten minutes. Flouring hands well (dough will be sticky) form in to small balls (about three ounces).

6. Place on a cookie sheet. Slash tops with a knife (to release air). Cover. Let rise until double in size.

7. Bake at 350 degrees till golden brown all over (15 to 20 minutes).

Makes about thirty love buns.

Church

Church attendance three out of four Sundays a month was and is a requirement for Salem Academy boarding students so they stay connected to the founding Moravian church. I belonged to First Presbyterian Church at home but I was now in an adventurous Nancy Drew mode, so I visited the Episcopal church, the Jewish temple, and the Greek Orthodox church. The congregations were welcoming but the language and liturgy were so foreign that I felt like an outsider. The Home Moravian Church was a two-minute walk from the Academy and since I was usually running late—some things never change—that's where I usually attended church if I had not figured out a way to be out of town for the weekend, the only acceptable excuse for not attending.

I had always gone to church. My father grew up next door to the First Presbyterian Church in my hometown, had been a member his whole life, and required attendance of my brother and me four out of four Sundays a month. Mom, an organist and choirmaster, grew up in the Methodist Church and after marrying Dad, became the organist at First Presbyterian. She worked there for years before moving across the street to become the organist/choirmaster at All Saints' Episcopal Church.

The minute we got home every Sunday, my parents started poking the white underbelly of church life and politics. Somebody in the choir was mad at somebody else so had stopped coming to church all together. Somebody on the Session (the governing board for a Presbyterian congregation) who did not get his way on the budget stopped speaking to the person in the chair next to him. Such irony for a place that was all about love and neighbors and forgiveness. I didn't like the ugliness in a place that was not supposed to be ugly and I didn't like that my parents talked about it for what felt like hours.

Even with all the bickering at church, the people who were angry, the sermons that went on too long, the youth event that flopped, we kept on going and going Sunday after Sunday after Sunday. We loved our assistant minister Andy (our Basset Hound's namesake) and the kind old members of the church who had known our family for years. Mom's hymn playing sent chills down every spine and there was something about singing those words with everyone at the same time. We were all in it together. My parents knew that there was no escaping messiness or disagreement or strife. If they quit the chaos in the church, they might as well quit the chaos in themselves, their families, their town, and every community of which they were a part.

I kept seeing that this is what you do, even when community and people are selfish and difficult. You keep hanging in because at the moment you peg someone else as selfish and difficult, you realize you are, too. And if you are not in community with these folks, all together, in one big pile of talking and arguing and singing, you never learn to work out all those selfishnesses and difficulties.

Here is what I had learned of denomination in my hometown: There were Presbyterians, (my family growing up), Methodists (my maternal grandparents), Baptists (my cute first boyfriend), Episcopalians (my family later and the people who drank wine at communion) and Catholics (the families in town with more than four children, leading me to reason that Catholicism had everything to do with sex).

My friend-since-preschool was Baptist and I often visited her church on Sunday nights. The pews were packed and it felt like these were the popular people. What could have mattered more during preadolescence? There were good-looking guys, big games and snacks far better than we Presbyterians had. All the people who carried around their personal marked-up Bibles looked like they were important, like they *belonged*. My friend's mom wailed *Great is Thy Faithfulness* on piano and people were singing and swaying and being saved and crying after they had "dedicated" their lives to Jesus Christ. Such a swell of emotion.

But something held me back. It might have had to do with that foreboding swimming pool down front. Why was it so deep? Or maybe it was all the certainty. There was so much of it. Definite heaven, definite hell. People who belonged, people who did not. People who were forgiven, people who were not. Despite what the Baptist minister was telling me, I did not believe God needed me to be baptized again, especially in that scary swimming pool. Granted, I had screamed through my entire Presbyterian baptism when I was a baby, but my baptism was no less legitimate. I was fresh from God, not yet marred by life, and babyhood, when I was still adorable, was a perfect time for me to join in community with others who vowed to care for me. That water on my head pointed to God's free, unearned grace. Most days, I cannot accept that God loves me unconditionally. That kind of love is too overwhelming. Then I think of that water and my baby tears. I am a beloved child of God. You are, too.

When it came to Communion, Jesus must have had other places to be most Sundays because at our Presbyterian church, we only shared His body and blood once a quarter. I was excited to walk in church those Sundays when I saw the polished silver stack of Communion trays on the table up front. When the sun shone through the multi-colored panes in the windows and ricocheted off the silver Jesus trays, the Divine seemed present, but that is not what excited me. What was exciting was the change in routine, the chance to eat food, even if it was just a little, in church. In combination with the lemonade and Saltines I had just been given in Sunday School, at least on this day my Cheerios wouldn't have to tide me over till lunch.

Communion Sundays were solemn days. The ushers, when they were not passing trays, placed their hands, one over the other, on their crotches. Our minister closed his eyes at the altar up front and told us this this was just like the Last Supper Jesus shared with his friends before he died. Sadness and darkness. Why did the sun pick now to step out from behind the clouds and shine through these contemporary stained glass windows, tall palettes of color blocks? This was serious, not a time for light.

After we all confessed our sins and brokenness and acknowledged we would receive this body and blood with our brothers and sisters in Christ, Mom played *Break Thou the Bread of Life* on the big Schantz organ in the balcony behind us. We did not dare leave our seats to meet Jesus at the table. We were Presbyterians. Jesus was coming to us. The non-smiling ushers passed the polished silver tray of tiny squares of unleavened bread pellets. I knew these squares to be unleavened bread but they looked and tasted like undecorated postage stamps.

We put them on the tips of our tongues and, like a Zyrtec allergy pill, they disintegrated. I couldn't believe such a tiny, tasteless morsel existed. Just like Dad, after I put the stamp on my tongue, I closed my eyes. I didn't see his lips move but I think he was praying.

Then it was time for the heavy solid silver trays of tiny plastic cups of grape juice, not a drop of alcohol. My hand shook as I took the laden tray from my neighbor, at once petrified and thrilled by the possibility of dropping the whole tray. Jesus's blood splashing my dress and the gold fabric of the pew cushions. Dad and I closed our eyes again while we shot the juice to the back of our throats. It was finished. We prayed and moved on with the rest of the worship. I still felt hungry for more.

I cannot claim some kind of sophisticated spiritual understanding at a young age and I am guilty, as we all are, of reconsidering history from my current vision and understanding. At the same time, I believe that God bestows our children, our teenagers, our young adults with a deep and powerful perception of the Holy Spirit's presence in worship. In their freshness, they might be more able to live out the flip-flopped, first-shall-be-last, resurrected life that we adults, so confident in our wisdom, can't fully integrate. When we hear of radical, inclusive faith that fills you up to the brim, we balk in our cynicism. *That's not the way the world works,* we say. *Why not,* they say back to us?

Blood

I never knew much about blood before I met my husband Mark and then it came spilling out all over the place. So red and viscous, I could not turn away.

We were dating in college, sitting outside together one night when he said he needed to tell me something serious. The mountain sky was filled with bright stars, but so black and dark, I could not see his face. Olber's paradox. As close in proximity as we were, I could tell only from the direction of his voice that he was looking down while he spoke. *I had a horrible wreck when I was in high school. Something so bad, I've never told anyone away from home.*

When he was seventeen, he was driving his Camaro at dusk on a hot July evening. Two of his friends were in the car and they were singing, laughing together. Mark arrived at a familiar four-way stop in his neighborhood, glanced up the hill on the cross street, and even though his view was obscured by summertime honeysuckle bushes, he saw nothing moving and so began to roll through the intersection.

In that precise moment, Mark heard a thud and the smash of his windshield. His mind raced. He knew he had not hit a car but he could not understand what had happened. Did I somehow hit a telephone pole? Maybe it was an animal. Did someone throw something at my car or did something fall from the sky? Beating heart, sweat. His car still moved so he peered through the web of smashed glass and crept to the side of the road. When he and his friends got out of the car, they saw a motorcycle on its side and the rider's body, bloody and nearly lifeless, thrown far away from the car. It was the boy's body that had shattered Mark's windshield.

An ambulance took Mark to the hospital to be treated for minor injuries. The motorcyclist was taken to the same hospital to be treated, but was pronounced dead. When the families of both boys saw each other at the hospital, they hugged and cried because they knew each other from the small Episcopal Church where they were all members. The priest from their church arrived to minister to both families.

There were no charges filed, as the police determined shared culpability with both Mark, who had not come to a complete stop, and the boy, who was riding without a helmet and going twice the speed limit. A tragic collision of two impetuous boys, one of whom was living, the other one dead. The facts, however, could not bring the boy back to life. The facts could not heal a mother's heartbreak. The facts would not change Mark's feelings of both responsibility and guilt. As Mark told me of his wreck, I wished I could see him more clearly. I wanted to be able to look into his brown eyes, but the night was too black.

Everything was different after the wreck. His friends at school were distant and confused, not knowing what to say to him. Mark had little interest in the now-trivial subjects they had talked about before—basketball, debate, prom. He began volunteering with a group of intellectually disabled men, playing board games and taking the men into town to get milkshakes. Everyone was familiar with one of the men, Jack, because of his frequent walks all around town. One of Mark's friends at school asked him what he was doing walking around with "that *retard*, Jack." Mark was shocked by his own outrage over this cruelty. He had become friends with Jack and now empathized with his outcast status. Little did Mark know, years later he would feel that outrage again when he heard someone refer to his own daughter as *retard*.

When I saw Mark the day after he disclosed his wreck, he said he was afraid I might run away. I assured him I had always been a clumsy runner, with bad form, so I probably wouldn't get very far. But I could now see how the blood had changed him. Most of our friends and I were thriving in a young adult world of classes, college parties, and overcooked dining hall food. Although Mark found solace in this same predictable world, he bore an additional burden most of us did not. He could not escape the crash, the thud, the absence. Red was so loud.

Now all of Mark's religion courses, even though he was an art major, and his devout chapel attendance made sense to me. While Mark danced with the rest of us on Saturday nights, he worshipped nearly every Sunday in the chapel and sometimes served as the crucifer who processed the cross. In this stone chapel he found peace. Here, God's changeless presence would not burn away no matter how much Mark doused the flame with buckets of guilt, anger, regret. He confessed his sins and heard the priest's words from the Episcopal *Book of Common Prayer*, "Almighty God have mercy on you, forgive you all your sins † through our Lord Jesus Christ, strengthen you in all † goodness, and by the power of the Holy Spirit keep you in † eternal life." He took the crumbly bread and port wine into his own body. Cleansed, he walked out to begin again.

After we graduated from college and I finished a Master's Degree, we married. Mark was working as an artist and I was teaching high school English. One day he picked me up from work in his gold Buick, called the *Buck* because the *i* of the rear nameplate was missing, and told me he needed to talk to me about something serious. Two times constitute a pattern. What could it be now? Was he having an affair? Joining the military? I placed my hands on the bench seat and braced myself.

*I feel a call to t*he Episcopal priesthood. This was not surprising, considering how much he loved the Episcopal Church, but my questions flowed. How does one receive A Call from God? In a dream? In a voicemail? There are days when I wish I had said, "Maybe you could consider becoming a corporate attorney, sweetheart. You're such a great debater." But before I even had the chance to crank down the car window for a breath of air, I heard myself say, "You are exactly the kind of person God is calling to be a priest. Someone who knows pain, loss, forgiveness. Do it."

Mark's journey to the priesthood was rigorous, as are most Episcopal processes. Before he could be accepted as a postulant, a candidate for holy orders in our home diocese, he was required to undergo background checks and psychological assessments to see if he was fit to withstand difficult pastoral and other demands. The Commission on Ministry asked both of us questions about our relationship, finances, and prayer lives. After he was accepted as a postulant, he was approved to go to seminary. Our first daughter Hannah had just been born and I was not yet ready to leave my home to move across the country for seminary. In consultation with our bishop, we decided to wait a year for Hannah to grow, a year in which Mark submerged himself in ministry.

He made and served sandwiches at a weekly soup kitchen. In the generic bologna, mustard, and white bread sandwiches, his compassion grew as he witnessed the emptiness and hopelessness of so many people's lives. He accepted a job as a psychological assistant in a wilderness program for adolescent boys with addiction and conduct disorders. Working with these boys forced Mark to face some of his own boyhood demons. Desperate for attention and full of misguided entitlement, the boys were difficult. But on the ropes course and by the blaze of campfires, the boys who worked the program became more humble, more vulnerable, less afraid. In working with the boys, Mark also became more vulnerable and less afraid.

He completed his first academic year of seminary and began his Clinical Pastoral Education

(CPE) assignment the following summer as an on-call chaplain at a downtown Chicago hospital. It was not my decision of course, but I was concerned this was not an appropriate ministry site for him. There were other safer, less bloody assignments he could have chosen. Places where ministry was not as blunt or urgent. He had worked hard in ongoing therapy to deal with the trauma of his high school wreck, but being in the midst of incessant injury and death would have to affect him.

After he had spent his first night in the hospital, awakened over and over by the pager on his belt, I realized why he was there. Mark believed that responsibility was not in turning away from earthly horror but walking right into the flame, towards the blue center of God. He had experienced God's presence in the crash and knew God was present here, in the gaping gunshot wounds, the burn of electrocution, the stillness of paralysis. Mark was not naïve. He did not and does not believe that if we pray hard enough, God will take away all the pain or save us from the wicked twists of our physical selves in this earthly existence. Suffering and death are inevitable. But through beseeching prayers, healing oils, human touch, we find God's comfort, presence, and power.

There are days when I see the haunting return to Mark's eyes. When our middle daughter first drove out of the driveway by herself. When he buried the ashes of our friends' three-year-old child. When our youngest fell down the steps and blood poured from her face. At first he is scared and he panics. Then he closes his eyes and prays for God's presence, power, and love to burn so hot that we have to jump back to avoid the sparks. Or at least run get some marshmallows. What I see then is not the color of his eyes but the red, red of his beating heart.

Greek Pastitio

INGREDIENTS

1 box uncooked ziti pasta

2 lbs lean ground beef

$^1/_2$ to 1 cup frozen chopped onions, depending on your taste

2 cloves garlic, chopped

1 Tbsp. ground cinnamon

1 tsp. Greek seasoning or oregano
1 15-oz. can of tomato sauce
salt
pepper

For bechamel sauce
2 cups whole milk
4 Tbsp (½ stick) unsalted butter
¼ cup flour
½ tsp. nutmeg
½ cup parmesan cheese
salt
pepper
1 egg, beaten

DIRECTIONS

1. Cook ground beef and onions together until beef is no longer pink. Add garlic and cook for 2 more minutes. Drain off any excess grease. Add cinnamon, Greek seasoning or oregano, tomato sauce, and salt and pepper to taste. Let simmer on low heat for about 30 minutes so flavors get to know each other.

2. While sauce is simmering, prepare pasta al dente, according to box instructions. Drain and toss with a little olive oil or butter. Place in large baking dish (this dish is tall) sprayed with canola oil.

3. Preheat oven to 350 F.

4. For bechamel sauce, heat the milk in the microwave or in a pan on medium low heat until it is simmering. Do not let it burn. In another pan, melt the butter, then add flour and cook on medium heat for two minutes, whisking constantly. Add warm milk to mixture and continue to cook over medium heat for about 5 or 6 minutes. Stir frequently until sauce becomes thick. In a small bowl, combine a little bit of the sauce with the beaten egg then add that mixture back into the bechamel. Stirring constantly, bring to a very gentle boil for 2 minutes. Stir in nutmeg, salt, pepper and parmesan cheese.

5. Layer the tomato meat sauce over the pasta then spread the bechamel evenly on top. Bake covered for 20 minutes then uncovered for about 30 more minutes until bubbly. Let rest for 10 minutes then eat with a Greek salad. Amaze your coworkers and take some to work the next day in your lunch.

A Way In

I am married to a clergy person so people assume I know a lot about the Bible. It's embarrassing how little I know about the Bible, but there is a verse from I Corinthians that I have had repeated to me too often when times are tough with our intellectually disabled (ID) and autistic oldest daughter Hannah: "No testing has overtaken you that is not common to everyone. God is faithful, and he will not let you be tested beyond your strength, but with the testing he will also provide the way out so that you may be able to endure it." Well-intentioned folks provide their own translation: "God won't give you more than you can handle, Martha." When I hear those words, I freeze. *What are you talking about? God does give me more than I can handle!* There are too many times that I feel tested beyond my strength and can't see a way out.

When I look to the text itself I realize there is more. It is not as if God randomly decides to bestow hardship—disability, cancer, death—on us. These are the natural occurrences of our existence. Quirks in our brains, in our cells. Instead, what I seek in this verse is comfort within the hardship, a reassurance I am not alone. That is, in most moments, enough. Hannah's disabilities have shocked and pained us but she is not her disability. She has taught us tolerance and radical hospitality for those who are different from the so-called norms of our culture. Daily, I pray to understand that our experience with Hannah is not our way *out of*, but instead our way *into* the world.

From her birth in 1993, all of Hannah's developmental milestones—eating, crawling, walking, talking—were seriously delayed, causing my husband Mark and me gut-wrenching worry. She was our first child; we had no basis for knowing what babies and toddlers were supposed to do on an ongoing basis. I clung to the straightforward British words of Penelope Leach, author of *Your Baby and*

Child, words that both comforted and alarmed me. Comforting: "All babies follow the same pattern of physical development but each one goes down that path at her own particular rate." Alarming: "By the time she is. . . three months old her head control. . . will be complete. . . ."

When she turned two years old, at the insistence of the director of the Chicago day care she attended part-time, we had Hannah mentally and physically evaluated. The director was worried over Hannah's major delays, the ones I did not want to face. She was not walking, not speaking in sentences, not using a utensil, not separating from me easily, not using the potty. Mark and I figured we could solve this, especially since he was in seminary at the time, learning how to impart faith and hope. Even though I doubted in the dark, during the day I was confident she would recover from whatever it was that held her brain and body back. With enough encouragement and therapy, she would edge into the "typically developing" range and we could all get on with our lives.

What I did not yet see was that Hannah was not a problem to be solved. There were skills she needed to learn, of course, just like the rest of us, but she was already a full, complete person the way she was. Her needs did not make her a saint—a special angel sent by God—but they also did not make her less perfect than any other of God's children. As with every human being, Hannah compensated her areas of weakness with fistfuls of strength.

For the next two years, Hannah saw physicians, speech therapists, art therapists, and occupational therapists. Doctors first diagnosed her as "developmentally delayed" and worked with her on every childhood skill that was supposed to occur naturally: eating, walking, toileting, listening, balancing, making eye contact, hugging, singing, throwing, jumping, running, speaking. We continued to work on these skills for three years, but her development still lagged behind and her tiny body would not budge from the meager fifth percentile of the growth chart. When Hannah turned five, her pediatrician told us she needed an Intelligence Quotient (IQ) test to understand why she wasn't fully functioning. Without a proper diagnosis, she would not be able to continue to receive the services and therapies she needed.

After Hannah's first IQ test, she was diagnosed with "mental retardation" (MR), a term from the Diagnostic and Statistical Manual (DSM-IV) used at that time. An IQ under seventy is considered "extremely low," and only 2.2% of the population fall in this category, but within this group are subcategories of mild, moderate (which includes Hannah, whose IQ is fifty-four), and severe. In the updated DSM-V "mental retardation" was finally replaced with the less derogatory "intellectually disabled" or ID. Now if we could only eradicate the use of "retard" from our lexicon the way it was dropped from the pages of that book. They are letters that never belonged together in the first place.

When Hannah was first diagnosed with MR, health professionals and friends said over and over, "IQ doesn't mean anything, Martha. It's an imperfect test. There are so many things Hannah can and will do. Don't focus on the number." I was grateful for optimism and high expectations of my child. I knew this was a number with no real reflection on Hannah's abilities. The IQ test began as a method of tracking possibilities for achievement in an academic setting, not for assessing if someone could become a kind-hearted citizen. But the world spins on systems that must be navigated and I had to work within established structures. As much as I wanted to ignore the number, I had to acknowledge it to provide the most care for Hannah.

Here is what an IQ of fifty-four means for Hannah:

She needs her fingers to add single digits.

She reads on a third grade level.

She can write three-word sentences.

She cannot remember there are four quarters in a dollar.

She cannot subtract eight from ten.

She cannot explain TV or movie plots.

She sometimes forgets to look both ways before crossing the street.

She cannot receive a high school diploma or driver's license.

What does the number omit? What are the components that exist somewhere above or below the number line, right around heart and soul level? Hannah can take care of herself—shower, pick out her clothes, fix a bowl of cereal, make a bus reservation, navigate the bus, get to work on time, work all day and take another shower when she gets home. She empties the dishwasher, cleans the kitchen counter, and helps scrub the bathrooms once a week. I can challenge her to find any item in the grocery store and she will find it, then send a text "I found it" before she comes back to the cart. She could go up against anyone in a word search puzzle competition.

More important than her daily functioning is her deep emotional sense, something not measured by IQ. She dislikes hugging and touching, but attaches deeply to friends and family who visit us and cries when a loved one walks out the door, even if it is someone she sees frequently. If you have a headache, Hannah writes a letter on a piece of notebook paper. "I am so so sorry you feel bad. I hope you feel better soon. I love you so much." We have a family ritual of saying what we like best about the person celebrating a birthday. Hannah chokes with such deep emotion that she can hardly speak and we have to speak for her. "I like the way you are good to me." She cries when she hears a powerful hymn in church, *Love Divine All Love Excelling*:

"Jesus, Thou art all compassion, pure unbounded love Thou art."

In 1998, around the same time of the IQ test, Hannah was also referred for a battery of autism tests due to her repetitive behaviors, extreme separation anxiety, and lack of social connections and appropriate social behaviors. She scored in the "severely autistic" range, but I insisted on another series of tests because I didn't feel she fit the "severely autistic" diagnosis. On these tests, she scored in the "mildly autistic" range. Since then, we have hovered in the middle.

I will go ahead and answer because I am asked: Hannah does not have Down's Syndrome. She does not have Fragile X or Williams Syndrome or any other list of syndromes typically associated with ID. All of her chromosomes are intact. It's just that her brain does not follow predictable patterns and her growth and development have been consistently delayed. She has only a small physical quirk clinically associated with ID, an unusual but harmless curvature of the fingers and toes known as clinodactyly.

I will also answer: I did not drink alcohol or caffeine when I was pregnant with her, though I did eat plenty of chocolate. I did not smoke or take drugs. I ate perfect protein portions; red, blue, orange fruits; green vegetables; drank milk and water; consumed a daily prescription prenatal vitamin with extra folic acid. I went to exercise classes with calming music, a gentle teacher, and a group of pregnant women who asked each other all the usual questions:

Howfaralongareyouwhenisyourbabyduehave youbeensickatallhaveyoupickedoutanameareyou deliveringnaturallywhatisthethemeofyournursery whoisyourdoctor?

Despite the many speech therapists, physical therapists, occupational therapists, music therapists, art therapists, psychologists, psychiatrists, holistic pediatricians, traditional pediatricians, developmental pediatricians, and developmental gynecologists I have taken Hannah to see over these twenty-one years, I still do not have a full grasp on how her brain works, what she understands and doesn't understand, what she feels and doesn't feel. We have tried twenty-three medicines—four of which she still takes—for managing her frustration, her anxiety, her attention deficits, and her insulin.

As much information as these therapists and doctors have provided, they can't fully illuminate the interior darkness she holds tightly within.

At eight, nine, ten, eleven, twelve, Hannah's tantrums were at their most fierce. Flinging arms, screaming, kicking, throwing objects, and all over something as seemingly small as a schedule change. Two of our many psychologists along the way have told us that fall and spring are the most difficult seasons for people with disabilities. Change in the air, change of the clock, change in the stars. Hannah has always been, in psychological lingo, "activated" in springtime. During this season, she is even more difficult to console and highly irritated over the smallest of frustrations.

When Hannah was nine, she was angry over something. Now I can't even remember what it was, but I was trying to reason with her. *What's wrong? Please stop crying. It's OK. Talk to me.* She would not calm down, so I turned, helpless, to leave her room. My frustration was simmering. Hannah's frustration was boiling. Mad that I was turning my back on her and leaving, she grabbed the wooden hairbrush from her dresser and threw it at my head with considerable might. That was the first time anyone had ever thrown an object at me out of anger and it was my own daughter. I was stunned. A pulsating, painful lump on my head, in my stomach, and in my heart.

At age fifteen, when Hannah started her period, she saw the unexpected red color in her favorite khaki pants and was furious. It must have been so confusing, painful, and scary. Upon seeing the blood, she ran downstairs to her room, screaming "NO! NO! NO! NO!" I tried to help her with the pad, tried to calm her, console her, explain that I knew it was scary and painful, but it would be OK. All the while, thinking, I *know what you mean, Hannah. My period makes me mad, too.*

My consolations obviously flowed through her like water, colorless and ineffective. While I watched with a gaping mouth, she stood up and tore the maxi pad out of her underwear. She held it up to her mouth like an ice cream bar on a stick and bit off a big bite. I guess the Always Maxi Pad was not as tasty as she had hoped. She immediately spit the remains into my face. A certain peacefulness came over me suddenly, because the white bits that fell from her mouth looked like snow.

I was shaky, shocked by being spat upon, so I turned to walk away. Hannah stepped over the white flutter on the floor and again reached for the wooden hairbrush on her dresser. Again, she hurled the hard brush at the back of my skull. When it hit, I was dizzy and wanted to crumple. I didn't even turn around to see her face as I walked upstairs to be with my other two daughters, Hannah's younger sisters, who were listening to the screaming and clinging to each other in fear. So much difficulty, so much frustration, sometimes more than I can possibly handle. But this complexity has forced resilience, opened my eyes to the soul of pain, and made me articulate what is important in this world.

After Hannah's diagnosis, I turned on myself and began searching for what I had done wrong. Like many women, I am expert at assuming wrong-doing and the associated guilt and shame. I had not produced a perfect child. In my expectation of some sort of perfection *which does not exist*, I was denying Hannah's human rights as one of God's children. Hannah is both as perfect and imperfect as the rest of us.

She is a terrible liar. Granted, that quality shows strength of character, but it also makes the card game *Bullshit* not much fun. Teachers, therapists, and our family all work with Hannah on game-playing so she learns the important skills of turn-taking, patience, counting, and social interaction. Hannah will, sometimes grudgingly, work on all those skills but she will not lie. When we explain that she can try to pass off three cards, saying she has three Jacks even though she actually has two Jacks and one three, Hannah refuses.

"That's lying and that's wrong."

"It's not really lying here, Hannah, because it's a game. It's actually kind of fun."

"It is not fun and you always say that lying is wrong."

"Lying is wrong if it's anywhere other than a game."

"That makes no sense. It is not right to tell a lie."

After a while, we give up and play Uno. Would that all of us had that strength of character.

Reading is important to me and it has been difficult at times to face that my twenty-one-year-old child who reads on a third grade level has no desire to read books. Hannah has taught me, however, that even though sometimes reading is a healthy escape, I cannot always use reading or any other introverted activity to evade talking, facing the human needs right in front of me. While I try to teach Hannah ways to be quiet and fill her free time, Hannah teaches me the importance of being immersed in the world, talking and connecting with the people around her. When I eat at the restaurant where she works, I am amazed by the customers who know her name and how much she knows about their lives. Unencumbered by restraints, Hannah asks people about their worries, their work, their families. Blessed connections with people in her world.

Hannah adores old people, maybe because she senses in them a vulnerability similar to her own. She is also very loud, which helps her communicate with a person who is hard of hearing. When I am certain I have been too busy to visit with residents at the seniors' home, Hannah insists we visit residents we know. We sit patiently, with long periods of silence. She does not mind helping them eat, or adjusting their pillows so they are more comfortable.

For many years, Hannah's best friend was Nancy, a member of our church. They ate dinner at KT's Restaurant together and went to see movies, always sitting close to the front so Nancy, more than a half-century older than Hannah, wouldn't have to "walk up all those steps." One time, concerned about Hannah's weight (affected by several medicines she takes), I suggested to Nancy that she not let Hannah order the "Byron's Favorite" chocolate dessert with its thousands of calories. Without a word, Nancy shot me a look that said, "Back off. Hannah and I will do what we want." And they did. I slunk away and never mentioned food again. When Nancy died, Hannah cried for days and can still barely utter her name.

Hannah, open about what she thinks, has taught me how to be unembarrassed. She doesn't worry about what others think or how they may judge her. When she was young, I took her with me to a lunch with friends at a restaurant. In one of the moments I wished her speech therapy had not been so effective, Hannah announced to the whole table and most of the restaurant that I had just had my "mustache" waxed so I would not "look like a man." My friends roared. It's not that they did not know or have their own waxes but in that Italian restaurant, the wax was ripped, leaving me exposed. I could either put my head down in my pasta or open myself and laugh. Whenever possible, I choose to laugh.

I watch Hannah in church and wish I had the courage to lift my hands and cry with emotion over the beauty of music and spirit. When I hear her say the Lord's Prayer louder than anyone else in the pew, I pray that I might have such strong conviction. And while we drink from the same cup, I pray that Hannah always teaches me instead of looking for a way out, to see the way in.

Target

"In the case of archery, the hitter and the hit are no longer two opposing objects, but one reality."[2]

(Eugen Herrigel)

Fifteen years ago, on a cloudy Sunday afternoon, when Hannah was six, she witnessed a hit-and-run. Being a little kid, she might not have paid much attention except that she was in the car with me, her mother, and I was the one hitting and running. No one was injured, thank God, as there was no one in the parked car I hit in a Target parking lot. After the long, loud scrape, I looked over at the red targets glaring at me from white plastic bags. To

---

2. Eugen Herrigel, *Zen in the Art of Archery*, translated by R. F. C. Hull (New York: Vintage-Random House, 1953), viii.

the toilet paper and Tide sticking out, I said, "I hit a target at Target" and laughed at my cleverness. *Hey, that was a pretty good one. If I drive away and pretend this didn't happen, no one will know.*

Like many things we wish we could do over in our lives, this situation could have been easily resolved, a minor incident, if I had just dealt with it instead of running away. But at the time, this hit and run, a sneaky act of self-preservation, loomed large. I couldn't deal with any more stress and I didn't want to face the realities in the back seat. I wanted to see Hannah at a center surrounded by rings of patience and kindness and gentleness. I had to look away from the target because all I was feeling was exhaustion, frustration, and guilt.

Hannah was small for her age, but she wielded power from her car seat, "Oh mama, you shouldn't have done that." A year before, she did not have significant language, but her words came together quickly with the chastising tone she had heard from me many times before. A parent/child reversal. "You shouldn't hit your sister because that's not how we treat people." "You shouldn't scream at me because it hurts my feelings and my ears."

Compared to our friends' babies of the same age and the hundreds of babies cited in my stacks of baby books, Hannah's development had not been on track since she was born. Her doctors could not provide specific information, writing nothing more than "developmental delay" on her charts after every visit. They were positive and encouraging, "What a cutie! She's going to be just fine. We'll try some speech therapy, some physical therapy, some occupational therapy to get her skills up to speed." Then, when Hannah was five and a half, her doctors and psychiatrists, not so cheerful anymore, hit us with a diagnosis of "mental retardation."

I'm a smart person; I can deal with that.

Hannah required constant emotional care. With severe separation anxiety, she clung to one of us, usually me since I was the one at home with her most of the time. Mark's work provided us income and benefits and I couldn't concentrate on anything other than meeting her needs—taking her to physical, speech, occupational therapies, psychologists, psychiatrists, and a developmental pediatrician.

I craved time with other mothers but we all knew Hannah and I were strangers, both needy and different. Hannah would become frustrated and teary over the smallest things. After a while, I did too. I had to be hyper-vigilant about all that upset, irritated or provoked her: loud noises, changes in schedule, scratchy clothes, sock seams, clothing tags, bright lights, crowds, anything sticky, feathery touches, firm hugs. She had trouble playing by herself and did not seem to see anything when she looked at a TV or movie screen. While friends of mine were struggling to wrench their children away from *Barney* and *Blues Clues*, I prayed Hannah would sit and watch TV for just fifteen minutes.

I worked hard to keep my struggles and worries over Hannah hidden from everyone outside our family. Mark was a new priest serving in a 3000-member parish and I didn't know how much or how little I could share with church members. I hadn't joined a support group because I wasn't exactly sure what kind of support I needed.

Most weekdays, Mark took over for me the minute he walked in the door and decompressed from work. On Sundays, his most demanding days, he led worship, preached, talked, and pastored. He needed the afternoon of the seventh day to be a time of rest. So did I. But instead of resting, I decided I would shop for household items we needed at Target. I should have known that going to a place where the cash register is set on $100 was not a good choice. Hannah wanted to go with me. I wanted to go alone. Mark wanted to take a nap. We argued. He won.

Hannah and I pushed our red cart through Target then loaded everything in the car to beat the gloomy rain. After I buckled Hannah in, I backed out of my space, turned too soon and scraped the car next to me. I saw in the baby mirror that Hannah jumped in her car seat when she heard the loud scrape. My overloaded brain told me to get out of there as fast as possible. I did not get out of my car to check on the car I scraped. I did not leave a note. I might have been able to run unnoticed but it turns out there was a sheriff's deputy who witnessed the whole scene.

There were logical considerations unavailable to me in that moment: It wasn't a bad scrape. The owner might have not even bothered to call me.

I had car insurance. But reason was not showing itself. I felt light-headed and saw black electric spots in the circles of my eyes. The heat in my face and neck was explosive as I confessed to Hannah, "Mama just hit a car."

I drove home as fast as I could. I was sweating and sick to my stomach when I drove in the driveway. When I walked in the door, Mark said a livid sheriff's deputy had just called and told him what had happened. Mark was calm but confused. As I talked, his confusion turned to pity. I guess he could see the arrow dangling from my hand. Mark said after he finally got the deputy to calm down, he told him I was going through a lot with our daughter and had just made a terrible decision. The deputy said, "Your wife needs to learn to drive." Mark let him say what he needed to say, then reassured him we would pay for any damages to the car. The deputy did not file charges after he verified that we had contacted the driver.

> "It is necessary for the archer to become, in spite of himself, an unmoved center."
>
> (page 5)

I had hoped that avoiding dealing with the crash would make it go away. Instead the crunch, the panic, the wrong, the guilt became more red, my chaos more illuminated. Women must drive all kinds of metaphorical narrow roads and I had found myself on one that seemed to be intended for bicycle use only. In England. The signs were popping up faster than I could read: Patient mother of disabled child. Woman who has solutions and answers. Self-reliant adult daughter. Cheerful, hospitable clergy wife. Christian who sees disability as blessing. Endless endurance. Unbreakable shoulders. Like so many of us, I was trying to incorporate all of the expectations and continue to hold it in the road.

Instead I was careening all over the place, in the grass, up on rocks, through streams and trees. I was tired and frustrated and wanted specific answers and a definite plan for how Hannah's life and my life with her were going to proceed. I wanted an easier go. I wanted to be taking Hannah to play dates instead of taking her to doctor's appointments and therapies. I wanted to be enjoying my time with Sarah, a typically developing toddler who needed her mother. I wanted to be reading books on topics other than disabilities. I wanted friends, both for Hannah and myself. I wanted a marriage that was not focused on the disabled child. When I looked around, I thought I saw everyone living lives of ability and joy when I was stuck in *dis*.

Since I had broken a law by hitting and running, I knew I needed a therapist. I barely let the office door close behind me before I spewed to the therapist that I had hit a car then left and I had this child with disabilities and I didn't know what her life was going to be like or what my life would be like or what Sarah's life would be like and how I would manage and will I ever go to Target by myself again and will Mark and I be able to survive this stress and we had moved so many times already and I was a terrible mother and I couldn't do it all. After my therapist taught me how to breathe, she offered three responses that first day: 1. A small piece of dark chocolate. 2. A mug of tea. 3. Not freaking out. She said with a smile, "Wow, when you do things, you do them big, don't you?"

When I finally became vulnerable enough to admit that I was confused, that I couldn't do it all, that I was scared, I was able to move away from the crash. Oddly enough, after admitting those truths, I could still taste that the tea was hot and the chocolate soothing and rich. I could still feel the blaze of the South Carolina sun that afternoon. When I climbed into bed at night, I noticed that the stars didn't fall, clink, clinking around me.

God knows the mug of tea was only the beginning. And since that time, although I have not broken the law—*do speeding tickets count?*—there have been repeat panics, times when I knew *this* time, the stars *were* going to fall. I have forgotten how to breathe and had to lie on my back, my fingers curved and my hand across my diaphragm, to watch the up and down for a good long while. I finally learned to tell people what we were going through instead of trying to hide my confusions and imperfections. Sometimes I talked for too long and listeners stopped listening. Other times, I heard "*Me, too*" or situations much more difficult than mine. I finally realized there were so many of us stuck in our *dis*es—our disconnections and separations—that I was not alone. I called the driver from the Target parking lot. I apologized and offered to pay for the damage. I practiced my driving. I shifted my prayers to God from the *why, why, why* to the *be with me, help me breathe, please may I have some chocolate?*

Photographs

On Saturday afternoons, my Dad used to develop his own photographs in the tiny bathroom of our house in East Tennessee. The counter was so narrow I could barely prop my leg to spray *Love's Baby Soft* body spray all over me, but he somehow managed to set up an entire darkroom in this space. After a week of meetings and deals and talking, Dad would tack a towel over the window and immerse himself in the pitch-black room, only a red safelight to guide his hands. He poured chemicals from skull-and-crossbones bottles onto photography paper floating in plastic trays. The room felt suffocating so I didn't usually go in, but sometimes I was curious. "Yes, you can come in and watch, but the door has to stay shut so no light gets in. Sit right there on the tub and you can help." The "stop bath" smelled like vinegar. I couldn't wait for the odor to fade and the pictures to dry.

From the black emerged images of all that was happening on Hale Avenue. Not much, most of the time. We have many pictures of my great Aunt Nell, God rest her soul, chewing picnic food, and photographs of our Basset Hounds in varying states of repose. Dad was as interested in depth of field, frame, and resolution as he was in subject matter. Validated and aligned with me, he was thrilled when I wanted to earn my Girl Scout photography badge. In our dining room, we set up different types of lights to vary the shadow on my stuffed animal Big Henry. The Magicube flashed and popped.

Even though I well know what Aunt Nell looked like after she took a bite of brownie, I still look at Dad's photographs over and over because it is the only documentation of the story I have. The details help me question myself—why on earth was I wearing a *Kentucky Fried Chicken* t-shirt?—and my family—why did my maternal grandmother, whom I adored, never want to be photographed? I still think of my experiences as scenes in darkroom trays. Pictures that teach me and move my life in a different creative or spiritual direction. Sensual moments of joy or pain in which God is, blessedly, present. Even when the vinegar smell is pungent, I can't divert my eyes.

Pictures.

After my grandmother, whom we called Maw, wiped out the iron skillet in which she had melted margarine and fried the bologna for our white bread sandwiches, she sat down with me at the kitchen table, painted her nails, and smoked a Tareyton cigarette. She did not smoke often but I can see that cigarette perched between her now-peach second and third nails, her head turned upward to blow smoke away from my face. Nicky and Victor talked in *The Young and the Restless* black-and-white background about their fifth marriage or maybe their seventh divorce. Maw and I talked about my own little soap operas—: how many Girl Scout cookies I had sold, why Debbie and I had argued, why my friend Mike had refused to go to the high school dance with me. It's contradictory now to say that her only time of self-care was while her cigarette burned, but it's true. The only time she stopped serving my grandfather,

rested, did something for herself. The first time I realized how difficult it was to be a bride of the De-
pression, how little women asked for themselves,
how much they deserved. And in that smoky moment, she was all mine.

My father had a business trip in Germany and decided, maybe against his better judgment, to take
the rest of our family with him. Part of the trip was
a meeting with executives and tour of the Siemens
plant, a business Dad was hoping to bring to our
hometown. Siemens had invented a new dental
chair, on display during the presentation. Mom and
I were the only women in a roomful of high-pow-
ered men taking themselves quite seriously. While
the executives spoke to us in German, the dental
chair kept going up and down, around and around.

Mom looked at me and smiled. I smiled back at
her. She tittered. I followed. She laughed. I laughed.
Soon we were laughing so hard the bench was shaking and the men were staring in dismay. Tears were
streaming down our faces and we could not get
control. Dad was, and still is, mortified. I always
knew my mother loved me but in that sterile Sie-

mens room, I saw she *liked* me enough to be vulnerable in front of me. In that moment, without even trying, she taught me that stress, fatigue, sadness, pain can always be tempered, therefore survived, with laughter.

When I first laid eyes on my now-husband Mark, we were sitting beside each other at the pub in Sewanee where we went to college. He was tall, with olive Greek skin and thick black hair. I know now that his eyes are brown but I couldn't have told you then because I couldn't take my eyes off his full perfect lips. He wore Levis, a light blue button-down shirt, and white Stan Smith sneakers with the air holes on the side. In that moment, although he seemed clever, I wasn't interested in his intellect, artistic ability, or his spirituality. I thought if I died right there, a mug of beer in my hand, I would have at least seen the most beautiful creature God ever created.

I see Hannah, now twenty-one, in the moonlight with Mark when she was eighteen months old. We were attending a family church retreat at an inn in Wisconsin and it was the black of midnight. Hannah, over-stimulated by people, noise, and activity became inconsolable, crying so much I was afraid for her breathing. We had tried everything to calm her, passing her back and forth to rock and sway and pray. Finally Mark held her in the same football grip he used when she was a four-pound newborn and stood by the window. He sang an unusual lullaby, *Yellow Submarine,* into her ear, his face touching hers. A moonbeam found them both. In that solitary moonbeam I saw both beauty and loneliness. Finally, Hannah slept.

Our middle daughter Sarah, now eighteen, wanted to grow up to be perfect. Sarah intuited, with help from me, that first-born Hannah could be difficult and complicated and she was determined not to be that. No fuss or trouble. She swallowed her plentiful worries. When Sarah was eleven, she was cast in a professional theater group production of *The Best Christmas Pageant Ever* as Claudia Herdman, one of "the worst kids in the history of the world" (the female version of Claude in the book)[3]. Sarah's typically neat blonde hair was tangled and sprayed

3. Barbara Robinson, *The Best Christmas Pageant Ever* (New York: HarperCollins, 1972), 1.

to stand up all over her head. She wore dirty, torn denim overalls, an exaggerated character to help the audience get the picture.

When she yelled one of her big lines, "It said in there [the Bible], they wrapped him in *wadded-up* clothes!," the audience laughed at the substitution of "wadded-up" for "swaddled." I laughed too, as the picture came clear. If Sarah continued to hold in all her fears, and anger, she would stay cradled in a stable of helplessness, pain, resentment. She needed to be wild-haired, wadded-up.

Don't you worry, Sarah. You go ahead and scream, cuss, stomp, cause a fuss, fall apart. That sweet Baby Jesus will sleep right through it. He knows that's all the perfect you need to be.

Elizabeth, now twelve, was born third into a vocal, opinionated family. When she was a preschooler, she had a wonder of bright white hair, rosy skin and a soft belly that peered out over her leggings, a belly we kissed and nuzzled. Her favorite shoes were a pair of Old Navy once-pink flip-flops, or *fli-floz* as she called them, now more brown than pink because she wore them in the rain, the mud, and the sand. All the time. Everyday. Little three-year-old, still learning. Wise Mama, has to teach.

On Sunday, Elizabeth donned a dress and her *fli-floz*, worn down to about an eighth of an inch, for church. It wasn't so bad when they were new but now they looked, well, disgusting. No, no, no, those aren't nice enough for church, God's house. No, no, we are the priest's family and have to look nice because that's what people expect. We need to start wearing the Hanna Andersson shoes that match, so your mama looks like she knows what she's doing, at least on the outside.

Mama, I wearin' my fli-floz. I not wearin' those other shoes.

But honey, look at Mama's shoes, Hannah's shoes, Sarah's shoes. See how we are all wearing nice shoes to church?

I don't care, Mama, I wearin my fli-floz.

No you're not.

Yes I am.

NO YOU'RE NOT.

Just like her favorite toddler swing in the front yard tree, back and forth, back and forth, until the swing got too high.

MAMA, EVER-BODY WEARS FLIP FLOPS!

WE ARE THE PRIEST'S FAMILY. WE ARE NOT LIKE EVERYBODY, THAT'S EV-ER-Y-BOD-Y, ELSE!

And then Elizabeth, in two wise sentences, leveled the swing and set me straight:

Yeah, wur are, Mama. We just like ever-body else.

"And the last will be first."

Dad taught me that bright sun will deteriorate photographs, that they need to be preserved in an album. I know he is right but I can't help myself. Can't keep from taking them out, holding them, smudging them with my fingers, rearranging them. Every single time, right there in the frame, I see again.

One Right Answer

———◆◆◆———

Numbers will be the end of me, though I hope my last one might be at least 100 as my two great aunts lived to be 102 and 106 and my grandfather lived to be 100. From memorizing my multiplication tables in the fourth grade to the basic math I took to fulfill my math requirement in college, I have struggled with numbers all my life. They are just so specific, so exacting. They lock you in a place with no other choices. I have never wanted to operate that way, instead choosing to view the world with endless possibilities of right and wrong, good and bad, and varying shades of grey, green, red, and blue.

Geometry tutoring might not have been quite so humiliating if my Dad had not been a math major in college. Dad calculates math for fun in his spare time. He figured out early on what a budget was. That word is so foreign to my vocabulary that I sometimes forget there is a "d" in the middle. This is radical, so pay attention: If you save money, you will not be out of money. If you do not have enough money to buy an Anthropologie dress, even in the sale section, you cannot buy it. I have never been good with black and white realities and often say to my father what I like about writing is that there is no right answer. He retorts, "What I like about math is that there is only one right answer."

Hannah has an IQ of 54. Those are the only numbers I have ever known that mean nothing to my Dad. Those numbers are to him what these letters are to me: To Prove A line DE parallel to the base BC of the triangle ABC cuts AB, AC at D and E respectively. The circle which passes through D and touches AC at E meets AB at F. Prove that F,E,C,B, lie on a circle. *Nothing.* Dad and Hannah are as close as lines AB and AC, respectively. They are as similar as 16 and 20, with 80 as the least common multiple. They love food, thrive on projects, create errands to run, and though Dad is profoundly patient, he and Hannah both find it hard to sit still.

For several years now, Dad has been working with Hannah on time-telling. He has a big old round clock and every time he sees her they practice together on how to tell time. She has not been able to get it. With her mother's genetic material, she probably figures, "If someone has already created a digital clock, why do I need to deal with all this big-hand-little-hand business?"

Over Christmas, Dad took his mug of coffee and sat beside Hannah on the sofa. The stripes of his rugby shirt stretched across his belly; the stripes of her polo shirt stretched across hers. Then, right there on the sofa, something happened and Hannah got it. Dad kept trying to trick her, but she could not be thrown. 1:02, 6:12, 8:18. She was right every time.

When they demonstrated time-telling, I cried— cried for her wisdom, cried for his patience, cried in the warmth of the divine light. When she noticed I was crying, she cocked her head to the side, looking confused, probably thinking "I thought you would be proud." Dad said, "She's proud of you, Hannah. That's why she's crying." That. That was the one right answer.

Mustard

In 1994, when Hannah was eleven months old, we drove from Tennessee, past endless miles of Indiana cornfields, through the South Side of Chicago, just beyond the swanky North Side and parked in the parking lot of our new home in Evanston, Illinois. It was a parking lot, not a driveway, because we were moving into student housing of the Episcopal seminary where Mark would earn his Master of Divinity degree so he could become a priest. Emotions aren't singular, but he was deservedly excited, finally heeding this call he had been discerning for years. He wanted to immerse himself in theology, liturgy, the sacred. I was scared.

For the first time since Hannah was born, I was going to have to leave her in daycare so Mark could

be a full-time student and I could go to work as
the sole wage-earner. Many parents do this, but I
was struggling with Hannah's developmental delays, feeling like I was abandoning her when she
needed me most. Professionally, I had taught high
school English and communications for a police
department, but finding a job in a huge city without knowing anyone proved very difficult. It was
still summer and the sun shone with intensity
through the single-paned window of our so-called
den; the icy wind from Lake Michigan across the
street would soon begin to blow.

Evanston was beautiful, as was the seminary,
so we were sure our apartment would be too. We
huffed up the three flights of stairs, opened the
door and indeed found it charming. And by *charming*, I mean *completely depressing*. I had known this
interior architectural style before, from grades one
to five. The Mid-Hillcrest-Elementary-School-Style
celebrates solid cinderblock walls and grey asbes-
tos floor tiles tough enough to punish anyone with
the nerve to slip and fall on them. Here, however,
there was no chalkboard and the kitchen was the
size of the girls' bathroom stall.

The oven seemed big enough to roast one chicken breast, if I squeezed. To be fair, there were only two adults who would need to eat and I was planning on eating out in Chicago most of the time anyway. Never mind I didn't have a job yet. Never mind we would be on a seminarian budget when I did finally get a job. Food has always been and always will be my comfort in any type of anxiety and fear. As much as theologians and historians might disagree with me, I find it hard to believe that Julian of Norwich was not eating an Ann Sather cinnamon roll or a slice of Lou Malnati's deep-dish mushroom pizza when she wrote, "All shall be well, and all shall be well, and all manner of things shall be well."

I felt conflicted. A bishop, priests, and a committee of lay people had asked me more than once if I was OK with going to seminary, if I was willing to support Mark in his call. I responded wholeheartedly *yes, yes of course.* That was true. I was happy for Mark because he would finally get to work his way through Hebrew and Greek, and share a new language of theology with his spiritual companions. As a lover of Mark and a person of faith, I wanted to be a part. At the same time, this was his deal not mine, and here I was living in a seminary where even the squeaks of the rodents sounded flat and Midwestern. When I attended chapel with Mark, I heard priests, professors, and seminarians speak of thurible, aumbries, and purificators. Too many foreign words spinning in my head. I longed for a return to the simple language I had known—bread, wine, peace.

After several panicky weeks, I finally found a job training trainers for the Chicago Traffic Safety School. I suppose my previous jobs oddly qualified me to teach teachers how to teach hung-over students of mandatory Traffic Safety School they should not drive after drinking. We enrolled Hannah in daycare and the wonderful staff began working with her on the skills she should have mastered by now: walking, holding a spoon, speaking. Her extreme separation anxiety, which later became part of her autism diagnosis, was painful and troubling. Even though I was grateful for the staff, I could not get past the feeling that this was work only I, The Mother, was both qualified and responsible for. It was frightening to open myself to outsiders who were now becoming intimate with my fears about Hannah's delays and concerns for her future.

We were all holding it in the road, however, and finally establishing a new routine. While Mark was attending class, reading tomes, and writing papers, I was traveling all over Chicagoland, training trainers in the Art of Traffic Safety. I was growing in confidence that the city's highways had become safer because of my far-reaching efforts despite the fact that many of the same students kept appearing in our classes. Then one day, metaphorically speaking, I crashed into my male supervisor,.

I was in the midst of preparing for one of my largest train-the-trainer sessions when my supervisor asked if he could observe a practice session to make notes and suggestions, common practice in the field of teaching and training. *Yes, of course, that would be great.* I was prepared. After I gave my presentation and explained how I would handle participant contents and questions, I looked forward to his detailed notes, the notes that were going to make me a better, more professional trainer.

The positives are, your content is solid and you have great energy! Yea for you! Then there are the negatives, some things you definitely need to work on. Tomorrow, at your training, I would like you to use more hairspray than you obviously already use. And your skirt. I don't care that much but I think your training would be more effective if you wore a skirt that stopped above the knee.

Now it is true that I do have some sexy knees. Mark has always said so. But I wasn't quite prepared for knees to be the center of conversation at that moment. I stared at my boss, shocked, not believing those words had actually come out of his mouth. If I had been quick on the comeback, I would have said something about the attractiveness of the colostomy bag he wore, the one he insisted on showing me in his office the first day it became his new accessory. I was too stunned, at a loss for words, but I composed myself and figured out what to do next.

The solution would be simple. After I completed my training, wearing the one navy business skirt I owned, I would go through the appropriate channels and complain to his supervisor who was a She. She would naturally be appalled and deal with him swiftly. I had, of course, written down every word that he had spoken to me so that I could prove the complete and utter inappropriateness of the situation. I sat down on the opposite side of her massive cherry desk and listened to her response.

Oh, come on, Martha. Don't make a big deal out of this. He's old school. That's just the way he is. He doesn't mean anything by it. He has been here forever and this job means the world to him. If you can't work with him, you will have to find somewhere else to go.

Uh, OK, so you are not going to reprimand him in any way or make any changes?

No, he has been here too long and he supports me; no need to make any changes.

I guess driving on Hale Avenue in Tennessee had not trained me for I-90 rush hour in Chicago.

It had taken me a long time to find the TSS job and we couldn't afford my not working while I was searching for another job. I saw on the seminary bulletin board there was a job opening as an attorney's assistant in downtown Chicago. Surely any job advertised through the seminary would be reputable, right? The attorney hired me so quickly I should have known something was amiss. He was kind, but always nervous, in a state of panic over the business, easily frustrated with the few clients he had and constantly struggling to get clients.

A few months in, he started paying me in cash instead of giving me a paycheck. Not that I don't like cash, but with access to some of his files, I found out he was going bankrupt. When I asked him what was going on, he became angry and said he could only pay me for two more days of work. On my last day, he laid the dollar bills and coins he owed me on the copier glass to make a copy and prove that he had paid me. He said I could leave the office a couple of hours early since there was not much work. Actually, no work. The sun was shining as I walked out on the street. When I got to the hot dog vendor, I whipped out my dollar bills, still warm from the copy machine, and bought a hot dog stacked in the Chicago way with tomatoes and pickles. Like my professional life, the mustard on my hands and face was a mess.

By our second year of seminary, however, life had become rich. Hannah was now receiving occupational and physical therapy and though I was far from fearless, I felt stronger because a plan was in motion. Our friends were solid as cinderblocks. I would have expected seminarians going into the business of spiritual and pastoral care to be supportive of our struggles with Hannah and my work and indeed they were. The spouses and partners in our community had experience acting as support staff and they fixed us dinners and shared movies. The head cook in the dining hall, just released from jail, freed me from my bathroom stall of a kitchen on many nights with his community dinners. I still make my green beans the way he taught me: —steamed, with a whole lot of unsalted butter and extra salt.

But I still struggled with my idea of The Larger Church. It was no one's fault, but when I attended worship in the chapel I experienced a world set apart from my struggles with hardship, anger, and imperfection. The grey stone floors and scent of incense steeped in muted wooden pews seemed too clean and pure. I understood the world of the Spirit needed to be set apart in some ways, to point us to something better, richer, deeper than worldly things, but I was still having to exist in *my* world which was messy and neon yellow. As I was gaining some clarity on Hannah and the person she was becoming, I ached to hear God's words of inclusion and comfort.

I answered another ad. You would think I would have learned, but the hotdog-in-the-sunshine experience must have dulled my clarity. Not only did I answer the ad, but the ad was for a job as an Episcopal church secretary. *No, no, no,* I said to Mark. *All I hear is church, church, church. I am sick of church. All you all do is read theology and you don't deal with the real world. Oh, and no, I won't do it. And did I mention I think I am pregnant?* Hannah had stabilized enough that we could consider another child, a balance to the triumvirate. And so it went. I was pregnant with our second child, Sarah.

Mark might have said something sassy about all the money we had flowing in and that we really couldn't afford to be picky and wait for our dream jobs with another baby on the way. I might have said something equally or even more sassy about how we wouldn't be in this fix if he wasn't in seminary. But only our rodent friends know that story for sure.

I drove to All Saints' Episcopal Church, the oldest wood-frame building in the Ravenswood neighborhood of Chicago to interview for the position of secretary. There were holes in the walls of the building. The carpet was threadbare and stained. Bonnie, the Vicar, was petite with a wide toothy smile and a guttural, energetic laugh. She did not pull any punches. She first explained that this church had a symbol, the Phoenix and its accompanying phrase was, "A Rising Church for the Risen Christ."

I could hardly get a word in edge-wise during the interview. *Martha, this church was almost completely dead. I have come here to work with these folks to bring it back to life and meet the needs of this community. Oh, and outreach is the most important thing we do. And we are totally inclusive. We don't care what people look like, dress like, act like. We are happy to have them here. And I love to kayak as much as I love to preach. And my dog will always be at work with me. And we don't have a lot of money to pay you. But you seem really nice even though you talk weird. And I really need help with filing. Oh and this is just part-time.* How could I refuse that kind of hard-sell?

My desk was beside a window with a missing pane. As the fall progressed, the room got colder and colder. There was a mouse who ran from under the window across the room whenever Bonnie's dog was not around. She might have been cold too. My daily work was preparing bulletins for worship and filing Bonnie's sermons and other papers, along with answering phone calls and other administrative tasks, as job descriptions usually say. While copies were running and thoughts were percolating, Bonnie and I talked about church, ministry, relationships, friendships, my pregnancy, The South, The North, kayaks, writing, and dogs. She laughed when I told her I demanded morphine at Sarah's delivery and it was as if I had eaten a cherry Lifesaver. I laughed when she told me to buy her presents for her birthday because she likes as much attention on that day as possible.

Though Bonnie did explain her theology to me, I did not have to hear her explanation to experience what this church was about. I saw it. There were people coming to this place not *despite* its brokenness but *because* of it. All kinds of beautiful people of all ages. They didn't mind the holes, the disgusting carpet, the peeling paint. In the church's imperfection, the people seemed to feel at home. I did too.

We did not attend All Saints' frequently because Mark was doing his field education in a suburban church. But I was there as much as I could be. As soon as I walked in the door, after I prayed that the frame would not collapse on my head, I observed that calm descended over my soul. I did not have to pretend some kind of pure perfection to be at this church. We were all, in a sense, laid bare and ready to rise from the ashes.

After Sarah and another parish baby were born, Bonnie preached about children and asked us to "remember with awe and wonder that babies are born, that *every* child born is created in God's own image, that *each and every* infant bears the mark of God." I sobbed during that sermon, finally aware that *this* is what the church was. Honoring every soul, no matter what, born in God's image, not set apart from this messy world but right here in its midst. I also realized this truth was not just this one building or this one priest, as much as I still treasure them both.

What I saw there and what I will see forevermore is that my church is about brokenness and imperfection. It is about peeling paint and busted out glass. It is about leaders who make terrible decisions. It is about leaders who make brilliant ones. It is purificators and hotdogs. It is grey and it is neon yellow. It is making copies and making investments. It is people who have visible disabilities and people whose disabilities remain hidden. It is the icy wind of Chicago and the blooming dogwoods of the South. It is both the sexist boss and the feminist one. It is the belovedness of God in a cold, difficult place. It is a mama, struggling to make her way.

Sarah's Birthday Apricot Scones

INGREDIENTS

2 cups unbleached all-purpose flour
2 tsps. baking powder
$1/4$ cup sugar
$1/4$ tsp. salt
$1/2$ cup chopped dried apricots
$1/3$ cup cold unsalted butter cut into $1/4$ inch cubes
1 egg, beaten
1 tsp. vanilla
$1/2$ cup heavy whipping cream
$1/4$ cup apricot jam

Mixture for top of scones:
1 egg, beaten
1 Tbsp. heavy cream
sparkling white sugar (available at cooking stores
    or from kingarthurflour.com)

DIRECTIONS

Make these when you are feeling peaceful and
happy. Scones are sensitive, a wee bit fragile, and
will sense any unease or frustration.

1. Preheat oven to 375 degrees F and place rack in
middle of oven. Line a cookie sheet with parch-
ment paper.

2. In a large bowl, whisk together the flour, sugar,
baking powder and salt. Using either your hands
or two knives, cut the butter into the flour mixture until it looks like coarse crumbs. It is important that this step be done quickly so the butter
stays as cold as possible. Stir in the chopped
apricots and coat them with flour mixture.

3. In a glass measuring cup, combine the ½ cup
heavy cream, beaten egg and vanilla. Add this

mixture to the flour mixture and stir until just combined. Do not over mix.

4. Transfer to a lightly floured surface and knead dough four or five times. Be gentle. Divide the dough in half and pat each half of the dough into a circle about 8 inches round. A pastry scraper helps with shaping. Spread the jam on one round of the dough then place the second layer on top of the jam, sealing the edges.

5. Cut this circle in half, then cut each half into 4 pie-shaped wedges Place the scones on the baking sheet. Make an egg wash with the beaten egg mixed and the 1 tablespoon of heavy cream and brush the tops of the scones with this mixture. This will produce a glorious golden color while they bake. Sprinkle some sparkling white sugar on top of each one.

6. Bake for about 15 minutes or until lightly browned and a toothpick inserted into the center of a scone comes out clean. Transfer to a wire rack to cool. Scones are one of the few baked goods that actually have a better consistency if allowed to cool. You have been patient and gentle this long. Wait, wait.

Meltdown

Hannah had a significant meltdown on the sidewalk of our church yesterday. Crying. Screaming. Stamping. I don't want to be with you! I hate this! My heart raced as I moved through Sad, Mad, Embarrassed, Exhausted, Sad, and Mad. The two of us had just driven eight straight hours back to Roanoke from the wedding of Hannah's Best Buddy in Kentucky. We were physically tired and emotionally drained. We craved the quiet meditation of the Gathering and raced to get there in time. Hannah prayed, sang, and sat in stillness. I could not settle.

I had told Hannah we would stay for dinner after worship, one of her favorite activities. Church meals are one of the few times when Hannah can exert her social independence, visiting and sharing a meal with people when Mark and I aren't looking over her shoulder. The problem on this night was that Mama was tired and wanted to get home. At the end of church, I suggested we go home to eat. I have known for years that Hannah does not navigate last-minute shifts in schedule, but I tried anyway. At my suggestion of leaving, she fell apart. Even when I tried to help her recover and told her we would stay for dinner, it was too late. She was too angry to turn back. Crying, she stomped to the car but refused to get in. People stared, wondering what was going on. Oh God, I thought, I am the Bishop's Wife. What will people say?

One of our priests, Mary, was standing at the doorway and I asked her if she could try to help me with Hannah. Mary made her way to the parking lot and approached Hannah gingerly, not wanting to frighten her. Hannah would not talk but Mary stood at a distance and spoke in a calm voice. My mind darted: This will scare Mary. She probably has other stuff to do. She thinks I am helpless.

After a phone call to Mark, I looked up to witness a miraculous moment. Mary was holding Hannah's hands and both of them had their eyes closed. Hannah sobbed softly while Mary, in her gentle voice, prayed for God's help, guidance, and peace. Hannah, who does not like to be touched, did not let go of Mary's hands. Like a blackened pile of snow under crisp spring sunshine, my own tears flooded my hands.

I was the one melting down. I felt stripped like a Lenten altar, down to my bare bones. I was worried what people would think and frustrated by Hannah's behavior. The rascally side of me—unsure, embarrassed, and mad—was fully exposed. But when I saw Mary and Hannah holding hands, I realized this is the way it's supposed to be. I do not need to try to shield my authentic self or my authentic child before God. The fullness of both of us—not just the half that's cheerful, friendly, thoughtful—is on that bare altar before God.

What keeps me wrapped in the blanket of this Episcopal Church is that it does not walk away. No matter the extremes of my own or anyone else's life, it stays and stands patiently with its gentle voice of prayer, mirroring the words of Jesus, Peace I leave with you; my peace I give to you. I do not give to you as the world gives. Do not let your hearts be troubled, and do not let them be afraid (John

14:27). This Church of mine wants me to be the most kind, thoughtful, peaceful person I can be, and it knows that is not the wholeness of me yet it still doesn't let go of my hands. It still doesn't raise its voice and run away screaming.

I pray that there are seasons in your life for you to melt down and expose your most core desires and fears. Know that God won't run away in fear or embarrassment. Wave your snowy brown branches honestly before God so that on Easter Day, you celebrate your own explosion of green and pink and yellow and red.

Easter Potato Salad

INGREDIENTS

1 bag of Yukon Gold potatoes
1 small chopped onion
Salt and pepper
Celery seed
Hellman's Mayonnaise

In the South, people take potato salad seriously. How your grandmother, your aunt, your mom— the best people in the world—made it matters.

Small battles have been fought over which mayonnaise, Hellman's or Duke's, should be used. When my grandmother, Maw, made her potato salad, she used JFG mayonnaise. Mom and I are Hellman's people, but I will not abandon my friends who use Duke's because it's obvious they need guidance through their waywardness.

DIRECTIONS

Boil the potatoes, skins on, until they are tender, about 25 minutes, in salted water. Drain and allow to cool completely. Add chopped onion. You can also add chopped boiled egg at this point but I usually haven't thought ahead long enough to have boiled the eggs. Add salt and pepper to taste. Add 1 or 2 teaspoons of celery seed, to taste. Maw wrote down her recipe for me and her last sentence was, "Mix in mayonnaise, and it takes a lot, at least a cupful for this amount. If it does not look moist enough, I add more." She knew it was right when it looked right. And it always was. Let potato salad sit in the refrigerator until it is cold and the flavors have had a chance to merge. Sit outside and celebrate the Living Christ.

The Academy

In 1770, Elisabeth Oesterleing, a seventeen-year-old Moravian girl living in Bethlehem, Pennsylvania, assembled some of the Single Sisters (the Moravian classification for unmarried or widowed women) in her community, packed some chicken hand-pies and *walked* five hundred miles from Bethlehem to the Moravian community of Salem, North Carolina. Oesterleing rested her feet and got settled for a couple of years, then began instruction for the first three students of the new girls' school in Salem which means "peace" or "complete." Despite the ragings of the Revolutionary and Civil Wars, a measles outbreak in the 1800s, countless stomach flus, roommate wars, and my best friend

Terry and me, Salem Academy has yet to close its doors. It seems peace *can* prevail.

In 1979 at age fifteen, I left my small East Tennessee hometown at the foot of the Smoky Mountains for that same Salem Academy, though a bit larger by then, where I lived for three years. It wasn't that I was a hellion (necessarily) who needed to be in military school or that I couldn't get along with my Mom, Dad, or brother Rob. Even though I fantasized that I lived up the street in the house with a circular driveway and sunken living room like the one on *The Brady Bunch*, I was content. And whatever we Johnsons lacked in excitement, we made up for in good food and humor. The defining movies of my childhood, much to the horror of my Disney-advocating friends, were *The Jerk, Blazing Saddles,* and *Vacation*. Although I could tell a good joke, my bizarre movie menu did nothing for my fourth grade popularity.

Of course we had the usual family struggles that arose from sharing a tiny bathroom sink and blaring *The Cars*, but there was no alcoholism, abuse, or poverty. My parents Margie and John are hardworking people of solid faith. They laugh, read, and, obviously, go to the movies. And they have, blessedly, never pretended to be perfect parents. They are not afraid to engage us and change direction when family relationships get snarly, which they always do. For that flexibility and courage, I am grateful. Their ability to move forward keeps me hopeful and conscious that no matter what, healthy movement and change are always possible.

My early life sounds like Mayberry and some days it was: counting bats at night, backpacking in the Smoky Mountains, and mint chocolate chip ice cream cake birthday parties. Other days, my Dad's bipolar mother screamed at him, insisting he was stealing her money when what he was trying to do was balance her checkbook. Dad never raised his voice to me except when he yelled, "Get in the car!" if his mother lost her temper during a visit. His tires screeched as she stood, still screaming in the driveway. And then there were East Tennessee politics. The biggest hitch in my *Andy Griffith* existence was that Dad was mayor of our hometown for most of my childhood.

Like all effective politicians and ministers, Dad was beloved and abhorred for his politics and decisions. A highly ethical Presbyterian (now Episcopalian) Eagle Scout Democrat, Dad has always believed in government's moral responsibility to build infrastructure and help people who struggle. Some of his campaigns were relatively calm (as elections go), but his earliest opponent ran his campaign from the downtown pool hall. Nothing wrong with a harmless Friday night pool game, but when gambling, weapons, and heavy drinking collide in a mayoral campaign, it's likely no good can come. Dad could not abide these folks running the city where he and my Mom had met, married, and raised their children.

This opponent attempted to smear Dad via editorials in one of the town newspapers, on the radio. and at public "rallies," which were political debates. I was ten when I attended my first and last rally, what I thought sounded like an event with carnival rides, maybe a corndog. It was, instead, a forum for thugs to hurl empty beer cans at Dad if they disagreed with him. Mom, angry and scared, quickly got me out of there and took me home to the comfort of our Basset Hound, Andy, who slept at the foot of my bed every night.

Dad received threats against our family, including Andy, during this campaign but couldn't ever be sure if this was just junk talk going around the police station or whether something might really happen. Threats most always work to keep people in a state of fear, but Dad had long ago faced fear in his own mother who suffered from mental illness. When he heard talk one night that somebody might shoot at our house, he didn't seem worried at all.

Mom, on the other hand, did not feel calm. She was not about to sit around and speculate on whether or not someone might drive by and shoot at our house while her children slept. Dad knew Mom was sacrificing her children's exposure for his political interests and commitment. So for a few nights we all slept out of window-shooting-range in sleeping bags on the floor. Rob and I imagined we were in some kind of *Wild Wild West* rerun. Dad has always seen pitching tents and sleeping in sleeping bags a big adventure. Mom has never liked camping.

I thought the name "Mayor's Daughter" might have had perks but I soon realized the title was not a compliment. It seemed to make my classmates presume me to be rich, prudish, and snobby. I went out of my way to prove I was not. I loved the snap in the air of Friday night football but there was tension at my high school during the day.

One of my teachers, angry about a city-county disagreement over who should operate the school system, started criticizing Dad and asked me, in front of the whole class, "Do you think you're better than all of us because your Dad is mayor?" I sat in that wooden desk, red-faced and stunned silent in the knowledge that my orthodontic headgear was no longer the most embarrassing thing that had ever happened to me. I had become *somebody* in this small town, at an age when what I wanted most was *not* to be different. Mom was livid at the teacher, the school, the town. Dad agreed it was wrong but reminded us once again that, "People are people no matter where you go."

All the simmering anger and Mom's worry about me got her thinking about the possibility of boarding school. The thought of my leaving made both of us sad but she knew if I was going to be singled out, it needed to be for what *I* was or was not doing, not because of my father's work or interests. I was scared to leave home at age fifteen but had learned from Nancy Drew that you have to strike out on your own sometimes if you want to become strong. That's when I found Salem Academy, in restored Old Salem, North Carolina.

Before my sophomore year, we packed the back of the car with Dad's 1951 Vornado window fan he had spray-painted yellow for me, some new clothes from JC Penney, my East Tennessee flat-*i*'d twang, and headed 233 miles over the Smoky Mountains to North Carolina. Both Mom and I were trying to be cheerful while we unpacked the car, met my roommate, and made up my bed. I looked out my window, watched my parents walk down the uneven red brick sidewalk, and sobbed.

Like any young camper, I was lonely at first but once I was there for a few months, I realized Dad was right. People *are* the same everywhere: hard working, afraid, committed, aggressive, resentful, loving, lonely, faithful, competitive, gentle, bitter, compassionate. They were all here. But my friends and teachers came to know me for what I said and did and wrote, not for my father's politics.

As with every high school experience, there was darkness. My best friend had a difficult childhood and came to Salem because her home life was so unstable. We are still close and to this day, I have never known anything like her pain. The school work was difficult and teenage volatility made our close community even more complicated than it already was. Along with typical adolescent highs and lows, we were constantly together and spun in a constant circle of arguments, tears, reconciliation, joy, and laughter. Our parents were not there for comforting words at the end of every day. Instead we called once a week from the pay phone at the end of the hall, our voices echoing up the staircase. The rules were strict. Five minutes past curfew and we received demerits. Now that I am a mother of a teenager with a driver's license, I understand why.

There was also bright light. We became our own type of family—whose members learned early to trust each other and help shoulder the burden. Teachers opened our sleepy eyes in small, all-female classes where we wrestled with literature, Latin, ancient history. Some Saturdays, we sunned ourselves on the loggia, baby oil slathered on our legs and tin foil up around our faces. Though I have still not fully accepted the merits of resilience, it was here that I first learned I must always keep at least a little bit in my purse at all times.

And on special occasions, our kitchen staff made us *Hello Dollies*.

Sometimes known by the less cheerful *Seven Layer Bars*, these delicacies are a symbol of the extremes of those years. Even though I make these rarely now, I still believe they are sometimes necessary for restoring balance. When your opponents are yelling at you or someone you love; when they are throwing beer cans, trying to knock you out; when they are calling you ugly because of your headgear, make a batch of Hello Dollies or beg someone to make a batch for you and leave them by your door. A good friend will know to ring your doorbell and run away quickly because you haven't brushed your hair or your teeth. Just don't leave the bars on your front step long because they will melt and you will be a mess.

Hello Dolly Bars

INGREDIENTS

1 cup sweetened flaked coconut, toasted (I toast
   coconut by placing it in a pan on the stovetop
   and cooking over medium heat, stirring frequently, until most flakes are lightly browned.)

8 Tbsps. (1 stick) unsalted butter

9 graham crackers, crushed, with some larger
   pieces remaining (so the crust has some heft
   and is not sandy)

1 cup chopped walnuts or pecans

1 cup semi-sweet chocolate chips

1 cup butterscotch-flavored chips

1 14-oz. can condensed milk

DIRECTIONS

1. Preheat oven to 350. While oven is preheating,
   spray a 13 x 9-inch pan with nonstick baking
   spray.

2. Place stick of butter in sprayed pan and put
   it in the oven for butter to melt, about 5 or 6
   minutes.

3. After butter has melted, remove pan and add graham cracker pieces. Toss with butter so crumbs are coated. Spread the buttered crumbs evenly in the pan with your clean hands or the back of a spoon.

4. Place the nuts, both kinds of chips and coconut over the graham cracker crumbs and pour the can of condensed milk evenly over the whole pan of goodness.

5. Bake for about 25 minutes until the top is golden. You can let them cool and cut with a plastic knife or eat them right away with a spoon.

Home

I could never send my child to live away from home. I am sensitive to these words, spoken to me many times over the years, because we sent Hannah, our child with disabilities, to live away from home when she was twelve years old. My reactions to these words are varied, sometimes relative to the deliverer. I first feel anger over the intrusion, as if the speaker has come into my home with a sharp blade and cut into my carrot cake without asking. How can we fully know someone else's life, their path?

For the longest time I inhabited guilt, the stagnant stool where I sat, head down, my feet propped on the lowest rung. Eventually though, I became bored with sitting and realized that the stool was making my butt bone sore. I was tired of glaring at the floor and needed to move. I wanted to be able to stand up, raise my chin and place all my ingredients on the table—the grated carrots, the cinnamon, the cream cheese. I needed to be at a table where I could be sticky, vulnerable, hopeful.—

We were living in a small college town in North Carolina where Mark had been called as rector of the Episcopal Church. For the first time in our nomadic married life, I felt settled, at ease. We had finally lived in one place long enough for us to develop close friendships and my parents now lived only a couple of hours up the road. At long last, I possessed one of the more significant signs of belonging: I had memorized the layout of the town grocery store.

It was time for Hannah to enter middle school. The words *middle school* can strike terror in the hearts of many parents, but the anxiety is magnified for parents of children with disabilities. During Hannah's elementary school years, I had worked with teachers and administrators to mainstream Hannah into the regular education program as much as possible. She was part of the regular education class for most of the day, only pulled out of class for a couple of periods to work on specific skills such as speech and reading.

It was important to us that Hannah be a part of the culture of her schools not just for her own sake, but for the sake of her peers. Hannah, of course, deserved to be a part of school activities and develop friendships. The other students deserved the chance to befriend someone who did not learn, look, or act in predictable patterns, see the world as it is. Not yet flooded by teenage hormones or clouded by prejudices, Hannah's classmates did not seem bothered by difference. For the most part, they were gentle and friendly. The school day was taxing for Hannah, but she was able, with the help of an assistant, to navigate the lunchroom, the playground, some of the classroom work, the playground, the bus, the chaos. Middle school changed all that.

In the pools of summer before sixth grade, preteens started swimming in their adult-like inhibitions and worries and notions. *She talks different. He acts weird. I can't be seen with her. He is gross.* The middle school building was much larger than the elementary school and the academic expectations, of course, heightened. Hannah's comprehension and work were on roughly a first-grade level. Whereas the elementary teachers and students had compensated for the academic disparity, the now-growing gap seemed to irritate both the teachers and the other students. Hannah became overwhelmed and her anxiety, always bubbling, skyrocketed. Within the first few weeks, Hannah was crying every morning that she did not want to go to school.

Although the school was legally bound to accommodate Hannah, I had to be realistic about what I expected and consider *Hannah's* needs over anyone else's, including my own. I had taught high school English and was sympathetic to the many demands placed on teachers. It seemed worth a try to place her in a class for "exceptional" students and continue to mainstream her for classes such as PE and art. I tried to volunteer as much as I could in this class, but unlike elementary school, the middle school was not accustomed to having parents in the classroom and they seemed uncomfortable with my presence. Hannah's teacher admitted to me she was, at age thirty-two, "burnt out" and needed to take off as many days from work as possible due to the stress.

Hannah stepped off the bus one afternoon and when she made it to the top of our front steps, I saw her glasses were crooked. When I asked her what had happened, she burst into tears and put her hand to her head. She began crying so hard that her words spilled out in a jumble and I could not understand her. All she could say was that someone hurt her head. I could now see and feel the knot.

I ran in the house and frantically called the school. No one seemed to know what had happened and my call kept getting passed to someone else. Finally, I reached an assistant principal who apologized for not calling earlier and explained that a regular education student had shoved Hannah's head against a classroom doorframe. The principal said Hannah had done nothing to provoke the student and that he would receive consequences. Hannah did not yell, but slumped quietly to the floor, her glasses bent, her head in her hand.

Mark and I knew that even though Hannah's wound would eventually heal, the scars would be permanent. Our youngest daughter Elizabeth is now the same age as Hannah was when this incident happened and I have asked myself several times what I would do if the same thing happened to Elizabeth. My answer is that Elizabeth seems aware, able to understand the precarious, sometimes dangerous nature of middle school, and is more protective of her own wellbeing. I would have been furious if this had happened to any of my children, but Hannah seemed more vulnerable. Hannah did not seem safe, her teacher was not in the classroom consistently and now Hannah was afraid. We faced decisions that felt impossible.

I contacted Hannah's doctor, a medical university specialist in developmental disabilities and we discussed some possibilities for her. *Should I try to homeschool?* He strongly urged against it. I was not qualified to teach Hannah what she needed to learn. The doctor had seen more than one marriage wrecked by one parent's being at home trying to do everything for the child with disabilities. He cautioned that my taking full-time care could have stressful implications for our whole family. Hannah had frequent, extreme tantrums that were scary for her sisters and exhausting for Mark and me. The doctor said we might consider a residential program, even if just for a short time.

Sometimes I wish I could write that I was appalled when he suggested such an option, that I had the strength to be a mother who vehemently disagreed with his advice and refused to consider such an option for my child. But the emotional weight at that time was great. We had two other daughters, ages nine and three, who needed a mama, too. Mark did not want Hannah to go but he acknowledged that even though he helped all he could, I was her primary caretaker. We all agreed that we did not want her to leave home, but she needed to be safe, to learn, to grow so we began looking at residential programs for Hannah.

The program we most liked was 434 miles away from us, in Kentucky. The horses-and-hills setting was beautiful and the staff, loving and energetic. We decided we would give the program a try, at least for a while. After we said goodbye, the rest of us drove back home, but it did not now feel like home now because part of us was missing. As we passed through West Virginia, we heard on the radio one of Hannah's favorite songs: Phil Collins's "You'll Be in My Heart." I was so dizzy and sad that I nearly passed out.

The structure of the program was rigid—a perfect fit for Hannah. I had always known how much she craved structure, but I had difficulty creating the tight schedule she required at home. I constantly struggled to balance her needs with the needs of the rest of our family who did not always want to be tightly scheduled and wanted to be free for times of spontaneity. Hannah's two wonderful teachers and role models, Rachael and Yolanda, (to whom I am forever indebted) monitored all her emotional reactions, her activities, and her behavior. They kept in constant touch with me and came to see that it was not Hannah, but her mama, who was fragile.

In order to beat the statistics that people with disabilities tend to gain weight, the staff explained their requirement that residents exercise every day. In condescension, I rolled my eyes. *These poor people have no idea what they're dealing with here*. Hannah's medicines caused her to gain weight and I had tried, unsuccessfully, every way I knew to get her to exercise. She argued, exploded, refused. When Rachael told Hannah she had to log thirty minutes on the treadmill every day Hannah replied, "Oh no!" and then got on that treadmill and pushed start, never to look back.

All of the small house groups ate meals together and even though the food was good, there was no sugar. I had always baked brownies, cakes, and cookies and now there was Sugar-Free Jell-O for dessert and unsweetened tea to drink. With the food and exercise, Hannah eventually lost thirty pounds, became fit and strong.

The House Mother was strict. Hannah was twelve-years-old and still could not go to sleep without her pacifier. We had tried every bribe and trick we knew or had heard and she would not relinquish. Hannah's new House Mother said, "Big girls don't use pacifiers. I need you to give them to me." Hannah did as she was told, cried for the first few nights, then told us, "Pacifiers are for babies."

I felt guilty about my respite but it was a relief to have a rest. There was no screaming, rigidity had relaxed and we slept without intense fear. I spent time with our other two daughters that they desperately needed, particularly Sarah who had begun to internalize all the responsibility and pain of Hannah's disability. Mark and I went easier on each other as we were less on edge.

After Hannah had been in her program for a few months, we attended Family Weekend, a time for parents, siblings, grandparents to visit. Under a crisp Kentucky sky, Mark, Hannah, Sarah, Elizabeth, and I held hands and danced in a circle to "Ain't Too Proud to Beg." We were in the midst of all kinds of people, all different ages, hands flapping, arms swinging, wheelchairs circling, voices shouting. Hannah danced so much she had to take a break and drink a sugar free lemonade. She was not used to all the spinning.

After a year and a half of her being away, our family had regained some stability, but we missed Hannah and wanted to be able to see her on the weekends. Mark was called to be Dean of the Cathedral in Louisville. I started all over again with the grocery stores. Carrots on the left, not the right. Powdered sugar on Aisle Seven, not Four.

Now that we lived closer and could see Hannah frequently, she was becoming more sad when we talked on the phone and more resistant to returning to her school after she had been home for a weekend. She missed going to church every Sunday with Mark, her favorite activity still to this day. She wanted to listen to the radio in her own bed, bury her face in the fur of our dog Bridget and eat sugar-laden pasta. She had not made much progress in her reading and math and was still testing on a first-grade level.

On Sunday afternoons, when it was time to take Hannah back to her school, she started pleading, "No, no, no! I want to stay home!" Every time she uttered those words, my heart sank. I felt stronger because I had gotten emotional rest. I had taken Sarah to therapy to work out some of the intense anxiety she was holding in. We were in a different school system now and the administrators promised me they could take care of her if she were enrolled.

After a year and a half, Hannah moved back home. She became a patient in the Developmental Clinic of Children's Hospital in Cincinnati. For the first time, we had the medical/psychological support we had been missing. A remarkable team—social worker, nutritionist, psychiatrist, psychologist, developmental gynecologist, nurses, receptionists—took care of us in ways I will never fathom. Cafeteria food tasted home-cooked. Hannah and I knew the layout: eggs and pancakes in the middle, checkout and tables on the left.

Hannah returned home with all her idiosyncrasies: changing clothes at least five times a day, carrying around bottles and bottles of Bath and Body Works lotion, shuffling through her Claire's ring collection. She was still loud and bossy, but I could finally see that these traits had less to do with her disability and more to do with her genetics. We saw the bright sides: the speed with which she could empty the dishwasher, the way she helped Mark at Lowe's, the way she lovingly fed Bridget at the exact right time every day.

This is a human story. Everyone in our family still gets angry and frustrated and anxious and sad. All of our life transitions have been and will be difficult because we are emotional, strong-willed people who crave routine and stability. The space and distance from Hannah, though heartbreaking at times, was also strengthening and life-giving. We now know better how to articulate when we need to go to our separate corners and breathe. We know that weirdness and complexity, though difficult, can be more interesting than predictable and shallow. We shed tears over fart jokes at the dinner table as much as we shed them over relationships. Hannah is back in church with Mark every Sunday she can be, carrying his Prayer Book and his crosier. Hannah will tell you she knows the pain of absence, the joy of resurrection, and the love of sugar.

Hannah's Buttermilk Pancakes

INGREDIENTS

2 eggs, beaten
2 cups all-purpose unbleached flour
2 Tbsp. baking powder
1 tsp. baking soda
2 Tbsp. sugar
3 good sprinkles of apple or pumpkin pie spice
2 cups buttermilk (If you don't have buttermilk, add 2 Tbsp. of lemon juice or vinegar to 2 cups of whole milk and let it sit while you mix the other ingredients.)
4 Tbsp. canola oil
Real maple syrup

DIRECTIONS

1. Beat eggs in a small bowl. In another, larger bowl, whisk together dry ingredients. Add egg, buttermilk and oil to dry ingredients and whisk until all ingredients are combined. Although you don't want big lumps, don't overmix the batter or your pancakes will be chewy and flat. Yuck.

2. Pour a tiny amount of batter into a hot, oiled griddle and flip when the top is covered with bubbles. When that baby pancake is ready, you know your pan is just right to proceed with the rest of the batter. Stack them with a little butter on each one. You know what to do next.

Nasturtiums

Nothing blooms in bad soil. In mothering, work, dogs, school, marriage, flowers, homes, friendships, and cooking, only the best soil will suffice: smelly, rich, black to insure full, beautiful blooms. In order to achieve such beauty, the gardener must exert, tend, fuss. Anything less will result not only in lesser blooms but sure disaster.

I was walking in the Maine woods, finally becoming settled and calm. As I breathed in the piney, damp greens and browns, the salty, fishy blues, whites and greys, I stopped cold by a stone bed of orange nasturtiums. Even though they had been planted there, they twisted wild and free, round leaves, a horn of a bright blossom. The orange was at odds with that placid place and perfectly at home too. Nature is kind to remind me, continuously, that right in the middle of predictability twists the spicy that forces us to pay attention.

I am not a gardener—a person who knows exactly what to plant where and when, a person who relishes hours in the dirt—but I can grow a few things. We have always been on the move so I have only planted container gardens with annual flowers, tomatoes, and herbs. This year, in the hope of more permanence, I planted pink peonies, hostas, and lavender. I also planted small nasturtiums in a perfect pot of Miracle-Gro soil on the back deck. There they would be safe from our dog Sammy's hind leg lift and I could use them in salads, or on top of the spectacular cake I will make any day now. I held up my green finger and gloated to my family when the deep green round leaves flourished over the sides of the pot. Day after day I waited for blooms that never arrived.

The nasturtium has the reputation of being one of the most effortless flowers to grow so I did no research before I planted. I now had to move backwards and figure out where all those leaves had hidden my blooms. *Nasturtium*, derived from the

Latin *naris* "nose" and *torquere* "to twist," refers to the effect of chewing the peppery, edible leaves and blooms. Though mysterious, the flowers deserved credit for having a sense of humor.

Nasturtiums prefer poorer soil. No, no, not possible. All the Internet wisdom must be wrong on this one. How could anything possible grow in sandy, light soil, the soil that you curse because you don't have time or money to haul in compost and make it rich for your tomatoes? *If nasturtiums are planted in rich, heavily-fertilized soil, they will produce plentiful foliage but no blooms.* I left my laptop to go outside and look again. Plentiful foliage indeed, not a single bloom. A soil diagnosis.

• • •

There are days I am a sharp, on-fire mother. On those days, I can become one of the offensive mothers whom exhausted teachers bemoan during their eighteen-minute lunch breaks. My youngest, who began middle school last year, was so miserable in the first few months that I was looking for any way to ease her preadolescent pain. Tears came to her eyes after she got off the bus and I couldn't stand it. It had to be my responsibility to solve middle school, make her life more manageable for her. The lockers were too small. She didn't know her way around. There was no time to go to the bathroom. She witnessed a group of students laughing at a sixth grader who had dropped her books. Her history teacher was, in her eyes, mean. Too much for a child, our child.

I spoke with her guidance counselor several times and took on her history teacher. I needed him to understand that his teaching methods were neither ones I approved nor methods any decent educator would choose because they were making our child feel less than brilliant. I needed Elizabeth to know I was supporting her. I needed the mothers of her peers to know I was a mother who cared about my child. I needed to quell my own anxiety about Elizabeth's growing up, my fear about her being in the world without me to protect her, my loneliness at missing her when she is grown up and no longer depends solely on me.

I listened to her teacher's explanation of his teaching methods. I remembered what it was like to teach school, how challenging it was to balance everyone's needs, grade papers, and eat meals. Her teacher listened to my explanation of Elizabeth's personality and what she needed to succeed in class. As a father, he talked about his own daughter's difficult adjustment to middle school. Elizabeth listened to both of us for the first three minutes and then wanted to go home to ride her bike.

Somehow we met in the middle and all three survived. After Elizabeth finished the semester, she told me, with a smile, there were times she missed that social studies class and the way her teacher taught. I think I shook my head in agreement and then, out of view, banged my head against the wall.

• • •

Nasturtiums don't like to be repotted. It may be an indicator of a need for more excitement in my life but I couldn't wait to repot my six nasturtium plants. I was too committed to my needy-not-needy flowers not to relocate them. We found the best worst-soil spot in our back yard, a place with plenty of sun, and I replanted the trailing vines. Sammy would be able to pee on my flowers now but that was of lesser importance. They might not even survive.

The sandy soil was so shallow I covered the roots as best I could and showered the plants with water.

After I put the hose away, I assumed a fake laissez-faire attitude in front of their round, green faces. *Y'all do what you want out here. If you feel like blooming, great. If not, that's fine too. I have some real work to do inside.* Quietly, I walked in the back door, looked out the window and rooted for those flowers. *Please don't die now. Bloom! Bloom!*

I casually walked by the nasturtiums whenever I was home, barely glancing their way, pretending I was just walking around with Sammy. They withered at first. Leaves that had been the size of silver dollars now shriveled. The vines that had been upright now dragged like they were lying on the sofa watching *House Hunters* on HGTV. I couldn't do anything but wait and make sure they had enough water, but even the water's effect was precarious. The soil was so bad, the water pooled around the base of the plants.

• • •

There are days when I am a mother who falls desperately short. I forget to put one of the girls' doctor appointments on the calendar and we don't show up and I get charged a no-show fee. I can't figure out a sixth grade, or even a fourth grade math assignment. I am too tired or disinterested to listen to Lunchroom Tales. I am late in submitting my guardianship reports. I have not been to the grocery store. It is cold and rainy and all I want to do is lie on the sofa and watch *Fixer Upper*.

I, of course, feel guilty for my weaknesses, even if just during commercials. But somehow on these days, my children find a friend who will listen to their locker stories, finally finish their summer reading on their own, and manage to cook for themselves a decent dinner. They have even been known to bring me a York Peppermint Patty and sit close by me while I am laid out on the sofa.

I am aware they might be rolling their worried eyes while they later text their friends that Mom is on her fourth episode. But if I pay attention in the quiet after I have turned off the TV, I see meaning and value in those days, as long as they are not the majority. By experiencing a mother who is not always moving the pieces, or trying to, my children get to practice being in control of their own lives.

A peppery taste of what it feels like to begin the rolling boil, even if the pasta ends up overcooked. With enough butter and Parmesan cheese, that pasta will still be edible. I see in our girls an increase in confidence because they witness their own ability to blossom in full orange, despite the lame dirt I have patted around them.

• • •

Resurrections sometimes happen overnight. On a sunny June morning, I was checking-not-checking my nasturtiums and saw about fifty new dime-sized leaves. The vines had all arisen from the sofa, found the remote and turned off the TV. All in a row, there were orange blossoms, wrapped tight like the towel around a child just out of a cold swimming pool. The next day, the blooms opened.

All across that patch was bright orange. Plants so happy they seemed to be laughing out loud. To take it all in, I let them settle in the sun for a few days before I started picking them. When I couldn't wait any longer, I dug deep for leaves and flowers that were likely immune from Sammy. I sat on the grass right by my patch and put the leaves, vines and blossoms in my mouth and chewed. There is no white cake yet, but my twisted nose knows my nasturtiums are out there, ready, growing like crazy in their perfect soil.

Elizabeth's Comforting Tomato Soup Recipe

INGREDIENTS

$^3/_4$ cup frozen chopped onions

2 or 3 Tbsps. olive oil

pinch ground red pepper

1 (28 oz.) can (any brand) whole tomatoes in juice

1 (28 oz.) can Muir Glen organic Fire-Roasted (this is key) whole tomatoes in juice

1 Tbsp. sugar

3 cups chicken stock

ground black pepper

$^3/_4$ to 1 cup heavy cream

Fresh basil, if you have some handy

DIRECTIONS

Saute onions in olive oil until they are soft but not yet brown, about ten minutes. Add red pepper and cook for about five more minutes, stirring occasionally. Add both cans of tomatoes, chicken stock, sugar, and black pepper to taste. Simmer on medium heat until the tomatoes begin to break down (bless their hearts), about fifteen minutes. Remove soup from the stove and allow to cool for about ten minutes. Then use an immersion blender (one of cooking's best tools) and puree the soup until it is uniform and smooth. Return the soup to the stove, stir in the cream and allow the soup to warm again for a few minutes on low heat. Keep your eye on it since it now has delicious cream in it and you don't want it to burn. Serve with chopped basil and grilled cheese sandwiches. What was once troubling will soon fade into soft, cozy hues of warm red.

Sunny Side

I used to make fun of country music. The twang of country, a twang I share, sounded too close to home, a symbol of small-town, mountain ways. And honestly, with song titles like *Drop, Kick Me Jesus, Through the Goal Posts of Life* or *She Got the Gold Mine, (I Got the Shaft)*, can you really blame me? No, I was a Springsteen girl, desperate to be sitting on the hood of a Dodge with a license plate from any state other than Tennessee. But eventually I had enough experience on *The Streets of Fire* and I settled down long enough to listen. I need to go on record, as I'm sure Bruce is reading this piece, that I will always be a Springsteen girl. But I have finally embraced the strength and goodness of my own neck of the woods. And it was, as it usually is, my daughter Hannah who guided me to The Truth. Hannah taught me to look beyond country music's titles, to reach into the music and hear the beauty.

It wasn't that I was unfamiliar with or disliked country-bluegrass-gospel. The artists who sang on the record player in my childhood home were Emmy Lou, Kris and Willie, among many others. Many Sunday nights, Mom and her friends held gospel-sings in our living room. Piano, fiddle, bass, guitar, harmonica. Songs from their childhood churches about trains, coming home, meeting Jesus. I didn't know the songs by heart like they did but I sat cross-legged on the carpet and listened, watched. Sad lyrics brought tears to their eyes. Harmonies and rhythms made them smile and laugh out loud. Pain and hope.

Roots are important so I need to tell you that the birthplace of country music was *not* in Nashville, Tennessee but in Bristol, *East* Tennessee, in the part of the country where I grew up. Bristol is unique in that it is one city in two states. Just like me, part of its heart sits in Tennessee, part in Virginia. In 1927 music producer/talent scout Ralph Peer set off on a road trip from New York City to the South in search of new musical talent to record. Bristol, the largest urban area in Appalachia (people who live in the area pronounce this word Appa-LATCH-uh) was the perfect meeting place for as-yet unrecorded singers who lived deep within the mountains. Mountains with tops still un-stripped, green and lush.

The Carter Family—Sara, A.P. and Maybelle, from the Appalachian mountains of Southwest Virginia—traveled eighteen hours over dirt roads for the chance to play and sing for Mr. Peer. When Peer heard their unique sound, he couldn't wait to record them. Not only what came to be known as Maybelle's "Carter Scratch" way of playing her guitar or the harmonies they sang, but these songs of lost love, hard times, meeting Jesus. Right there on the third floor of the Taylor-Christian Hat and Glove Company in downtown Bristol, he recorded six Carter Family songs, among them *The Wandering Boy; Single Girl, Married Girl* and The *Storms Are On the Ocean.* Songs of hardship, loss and hope; born in churches, on front porches, by blazing bonfires. Songs as prayers. Songs as means of survival.

The residential school where our oldest daughter Hannah lived for a while holds a big Family Weekend every year in the fall. This place for people with intellectual disabilities, like schools and colleges all over, planned an abundance of activities—a parade, fishing, baseball, fireworks, a dance—over the three days. The students worked hard practicing hospitality—saying hello, directing folks where to go, trying to keep their parents, grandparents, aunts, uncles, cousins in line. The families, bless their hearts, provided an abundance of emotion—nervousness, sadness, joy. All of this activity and emotion collided in a spectacular frenzy that left all community members elated and exhausted long after the last dance song played on the stereo.

We missed Hannah and were excited to see her. We were nervous about how she would be adjusting. We thought she might be angry about being away from us. We were heartbroken that our reality was such that she needed to be here for the time being. We were hopeful because she had already made such strides in independence. We were relieved she was in a safe, loving environment, with staff and residents who did not judge her for the person she was.

Aside from the games and the dance, the biggest and most important event of the weekend was the talent show on Saturday night. This show, like all talent shows, was not just a way to entertain, but a means of demonstrating the individuality of the performers. School staff *asked* residents what they wanted to perform and gave them options—singing, dancing, reading, signing a song, playing the piano. *Asking* might not seem like a big deal in a world where some of us get to make our own choices most of the time. But a world of choices is often not the reality for people with disabilities. Our family, even subconsciously, had fallen into this line of thinking that by making all the choices for Hannah, by telling her what to do, we would keep her safe and help her be the best person she could be. We, with our IQs above 70, were the superior ones with the wisdom and the experience. Do you hear God laughing?

Hannah's teacher Rachael had always taken it upon herself to give her students a proper musical education, from Pearl Jam to John Mayer. Daily she played songs for Hannah and her other students, taught them the lyrics and the tunes. Hannah had always enjoyed music before she had left home, but had not shown particular interest in a type of music other than radio pop. Along with Rachael, Hannah also attached herself to a motherly staff member, Yolanda. Yolanda was a country music fan and played country music for Hannah on car and bus trips into town or on other excursions. Unbeknownst to us, Hannah learned every single word to the major country songs of 2004. So, when Rachael and Yolanda asked Hannah what she would like to perform for the Talent Show, Hannah did not hesitate. Kenny Chesney's country song, *When the Sun Goes Down*.

Residents lived on campus year-round, so preparation for the Talent Show began far in advance of Family Weekend. The staff's preparatory work was mindboggling. First, deciding what everyone wanted to perform, then teaching music, lyrics and dance steps. Finding costumes that wouldn't scratch or itch and practicing practicing practicing. Day after day, month after month, so the performers would not be quite as anxious when the gym was filled with their families and the faces of strangers instead of their friends.

My parents, Mark, Sarah, Elizabeth and I arrived in the gym early that evening so we could sit close to the stage. We wanted to see Hannah and we wanted her to see us, cheering her on. Along with two hundred or so parents and relatives, we clapped and tapped to every kind of song and dance imaginable. The doors were open to ease the heat. Music and voices flowed out into the soft Kentucky wind.

After the sun went down, our girl Hannah stood up on the stage by herself and sang *When the Sun Goes Down* in her deep, throaty voice. As she held the microphone and listened to the karaoke music for her tune, one of her blue-jeaned legs moved back and forth. Although she was nervous, the more she sang, it was clear she was groovin', feelin' alright. For Hannah, Kenny's song, like many country songs, had a rhythm that was comforting and safe, lyrics that were cheerful and uncomplicated. Singing this song, a song she chose for herself, was a way to say to herself and to us, "I know what makes me happy and I can do this." When the song came to an end, a huge smile crossed her face, a smile we had not seen in a long time. The audience whooped, hollered and screamed her name.

137

She came down off the stage to sit with us. When everyone said, "Hannah, you did a great job!," she responded, "Yeah, I did."

The emotions of that weekend were overwhelming much of the time but there were several realizations that clanged up against my head and heart like a 9" Lodge Iron Skillet. Hannah became, in the moment she sang, a metaphor for country music itself. Songs that might seem simple on the outside were actually full of complex harmonies, voices and strumming. Her song selection showed me some of what she had been missing at home. She needed an appropriate way to express her moments of pain and sadness. She needed to struggle with some of her own decisions. She needed her own form of comfort and prayer, not just the type I wielded over her head as her mother. She needed the space to become her own person, be the individual God wants her to be.

When Hannah eventually came home to live again, she brought her love of country music, with all the singers who made it possible. Tim McGraw, Faith Hill, Kenny Chesney, Carrie Underwood, Dolly Parton, Reba McIntire, Keith Urban came right in through our garage door like they had known us forever, like they didn't even mind the dog hair, the laundry piled up, the magazines all over the coffee table. They brought their guitars and hats, their metal belt buckles and ripped blue jeans, their tall hair and big boobs, their red lipstick and smiles. And they kept on singing. Even when I was too tired, ready to fall over, they still sang.

Whenever Hannah gets frustrated now, she goes downstairs to her bedroom, finds her country music station on the radio, sits on her bed, and sings and sings. Even if she can't access the precise words or thoughts she needs to express her pain, her frustrations, her sadness, these country singers seem to help her with that hard work. After thirty minutes or an hour, she emerges calmer, more centered, ready to take the stage. She knows that times will be hard, that we will say goodbye and we will meet again. She finds, over and over, the sunny side of life.

Gapers' Block

was shocked when I was first driving in Chicago and heard the radio announcers talk about the "gapers' blocks" on the Dan Ryan Expressway. "Gapers' blocks" are places where traffic is blocked because drivers have slowed down to gape at wrecks. In the South, even if we gawk at disaster, we don't *talk about* it, because that would be crass and God knows there is nothing worse than crass. Chicagoans tend to value honesty and practicality over delicacy, so they take a different approach: *We know everybody is looking so we might as well provide drivers with alternate routes.* Just because I didn't articulate it did not make me less of a gaper. The Chicago drivers and I were at once scared, relieved, energized, horrified, and fascinated by the wreckage. A car crash of contradictions. Sometimes, we find our own clergy family at the center of the gapers' block, the one being watched.

Mark and I chose our clergy family life and even on days when it is complicated—OK, every day—I am grateful for the attempt at a deeper, richer life. We receive compassion and kindness from parishioners. As a spiritual community, we experience intimacy that comes only from grieving over a loss and joy in the celebration of a birth. I understood from the beginning that Mark's ministry was not a desk job but a way of being—one that would travel with us to the beach, eat a Sloppy Joe at dinner, even go to school with our girls. Having grown up in the church, I was not naïve about expectations for the female clergy spouse, even if those expectations were not stated on paper.

Though not every clergy spouse does or should, I have my own relationship with our Episcopal Church so there is some seamlessness between my beliefs and existence and Mark's life in the church. In most cases, as I have tried to respect parish members; they have, at least on the surface, seemed to respect me back. I have found friends in each of his congregations, women who help me navigate the waters of expectation that do not recede no matter how far into the feminist future we try to paddle. Women who understand I cannot be at every luncheon, that my children might not be scrubbed, that I do not pray all the time. Women who understand that sometimes my seam must rip, that I must talk about movies and food instead of church, church, church.

There are, for the clergy spouse, however, forever watchful eyes. I have been told my dress is too low cut (it was not). I have been told I am too proper (I am proper enough). I have been told my skirt is wrinkled (it was). I have been told that my clothes are "too much fun" (I would hope). I have been asked why I do not have a panty line (Spanx, but I quickly got over that and by the way, I can't stand the word *panty*). I have been asked what it's like to have sex with a priest (too many clever responses to list).

In the same way my teachers criticized my father's decisions when I was in high school, parishioners have criticized my husband directly to members of our family or to others who would surely deliver the message. During one church coffee hour, while my young children were running around, I overheard a group of men talking about my husband and a decision of his, with which they vehemently disagreed. I tried to block their words but the space was too small, their words too clear. With a red face and shaking hands, I asked the men to please stop talking about my husband in front of my children. They were not pleased. One harrumphed, "WELL! I see who wears the pants in *your* family!" (I do indeed like to wear pants). The community was angry with me for daring to speak to a parishioner that way. I was angry about the public ugliness. Disagreements are a given in every community, but in that moment our family became public property, marred by the reckless driving of hurtful words.

Not all communities are meant for all people. Mark and I came to realize that the pants-wearing church was not aligned with his vision of ministry and our family needed to be in a place where kindness on both sides was not a struggle. We moved on to another place and they moved on to another priest.

Commitment to ministry involves leadership, which is an ongoing battery of skills, and strong leadership always brings conflict at some point. Individuals or a group of parishioners will be offended by the actions or decisions of the person leading the church. Clergy spouses, like all humans, must develop a degree of thick skin for survival in church, just as in any other community. A crash occurs, however, when discourse loses civility, when anger and frustration pour out on the street and stain the folks who are along for the ride.

Our daughters have their own experience with clergy family life. From the time our children were born, parishioners seemed to relish telling us how wild preachers' or priests' kids (PKs) are. There is even a Lifetime Network show called *Preachers' Daughters* that celebrates the downfall of clergy daughters (notably, no mention of sons). With gaping mouths, we (I watched several episodes for research) watch as the teenage/young adult girls argue, get drunk, get pregnant. There seems to be an expectation that PKs, more than other kids, will live lives of purity and the girls' downfall allows gapers to point to the hypocrisy of Christianity. A more accurate Christian expectation, however, is that PKs would lead lives of kindness, grace, and compassion, but those qualities must not be titillating enough to inspire top ratings.

It's true that priests should be role models, responsible for guiding congregations in The Way of the Gospel. The Way, however, is not about Perfection either for themselves or for their families. Episcopal priests make ordination vows "to love and serve the people. . . , caring alike for young and old, strong and weak, rich and poor. . . to preach, to declare God's forgiveness to penitent sinners, to pronounce God's blessing, to share in the administration of Holy Baptism and in the celebration of the mysteries of Christ's Body and Blood. . . ."[4]

Heavy weight indeed for this person, called by God, selected and trusted by the church to live a life centered on God, Scripture and prayer. But this centering in no way negates the priest's humanness, which he or she acknowledges when he or she takes Communion with the rest of us. Together we pray, eat, drink and begin again. With the rest of us,

---

4. The Book of Common Prayer, "The Ordination of a Priest," 531.

the priest will fail but she will also lead, inspire, do good in the world.

The complications of clergy families and expectations might beg the question, *why bother*? As much as I love Mark, I could just decide to remove myself from church communities (that, in and of itself, would inspire some whispering), and support him to the best of my ability, as anyone else supports her spouse. But my staying in this role and in this church is not solely related to Mark.

In an ironic twist, it is in this Christian community, where I have become angry, where I have judged, where people have been angry with me, where I have been judged, that I have learned a way of living not replicated anywhere else. Whether we are part of a church or not, we cannot, unless we move off the human grid, remove ourselves from communities. Communities are made up of people who love and support us, of naysayers and critics. What the church, in its ancient-contemporary wisdom, offers us is a model, a way to practice over and over and over how to exist in community, how to move past the inevitable mistakes towards forgiveness and redemption.

For those who eschew the church community for a spiritual life in the woods, with a book, on the beach, I say *me, too.* Sometimes I am tired of my church family and need the wilds of the world to regain my footing. But I would also say that more is required for survival in this car crash where we often find ourselves.

I cannot figure out this difficult world, these complicated human relationships by myself. I must worship beside people, hear their faint breathing, see their ruddy cheeks, hold their dry hands, study the lines of their necks, bump their shoulders, listen to their autistic screeches to make any sense of it all. Their panty lines, their bald heads, their wrinkled skirts, their exposed cleavage, their tattoos, their tight pants, their overweight, their underweight is just the stuff that makes us stare, gives us something to talk about when we are tired. And it is the stuff that falls away when we move toward the front of the nave, toward Christ, and meet at The Table.

All I know to do when I pass a wreck is pray for a compassionate heart. Pray for the ones who have crashed by the side of the road; for the police, the firefighters, the EMTs who pull from the wreckage; for the nurses and doctors who tend and heal; for the priest who blesses; for the priest who buries; for the relieved families; for the despondent families; for the terrified gapers. I pray we remember we are just human beings, at once scared, relieved, energized, horrified, and fascinated. I pray for God's mercy on all of us. I pray that we come to The Table, in all our beauty, and share the Feast of Love.